THE ELEPHANT IN THE CHURCH

For my sisters, Eithne, Olive, Marjorie and Eileen, who saw me from darkness to light.

Mary T. Malone

The Elephant in the Church

A Woman's Tract for Our Times

the columba press

First published in 2014 by
the columba press
55A Spruce Avenue,
Stillorgan Industrial Park,
Blackrock, Co. Dublin

Cover design by Redrattledesign.com
Cover image *Mary of Magdela 'Apostle to the Apostles'* by Emer O'Boyle
Origination by The Columba Press
Printed by Bell & Bain Ltd

ISBN 978 1 78218 132 3

Contents

Introduction   vii

Catholic Woman/Woman Catholic   1

Women and Scripture   13

Women and Monasticism in the
Fourth Century   29

The Medieval Women Mystics   51

The Beguines   73

Lone Mystics   93

Women and Missions   113

The Marian Influence   135

The Sixties: Vatican II and Feminism   149

The Once and Future Church   167

A Word about Sources   173

Introduction

I attended a conference recently where I was constantly tempted to stand up and say, 'Excuse me, my name is Mrs Elephant and I am the elephant in this room.' One of the morning's discussions had to do with the absolutely egalitarian nature of Trinitarian relationships, of Father, Son, and male Holy Spirit, and the quality of absolute intimacy that prevailed in this three-fold community. I am accustomed to closing down part of my mind as this kind of discourse happens, but on this occasion, I realised with a new certainty that if females are absolutely excluded from this absolutely egalitarian and intimate male relationship then the whole metaphor makes absolutely no sense except as an idolatrous construct. I am, of course, aware of the usual response about metaphorical phrases, but this language is usually used, even by professional theologians, as if it literally denoted three male persons.

I use the word 'females' intentionally in the above paragraph. It is perfectly possible to add 'feminine' traits to these male characters, thus making them nicer and perhaps more merciful men, but they are still men. On the other hand, it is absolutely impossible – that word again – to interpose a full-blooded female anywhere into this relationship, because females still remain at the furthest remove from the traditional Christian image of God. So the whole system works perfectly as long as women's persons, voices and contributions are completely ignored. All the commentaries on the fiftieth anniversary of the Second Vatican

Council studiously avoid the issue of women. In recent interviews, women are the topic on which Pope Francis has least to say, except to indicate that he is fearful of feminists, or 'female machismo' as he terms it. It is a wholly male discussion of a male church, with a male conciliar tradition and also a male-dominant renewal. There is an occasional nod towards the generic laity and the ordination of women. The full realisation that this is not going to happen is widely articulated, as also by Pope Francis, and even if it did, it would simply result in women being admitted to the patriarchate in their customary subordinate and invisible role. So women remain as the elephant in the church, even though it is obvious to all that the men's church is in deep trouble and in danger of lurching back to the safety of the Tridentine Church of the sixteenth century. Even if the Catholic Church lurched back to the sixties and Vatican II, it would still be a woman-free zone in terms of leadership, ministry and theological input. It is well to remember the words of Pope John XXIII, to whom the words 'blessed' and 'beloved' are customarily added. When, as pope, he described the influences on his priestly life, he remarked that the most important advice came from his bishop, who told him to live 'as if there were no women in the world', and that he had studiously followed this advice all his life. It is a true template for church practice then and now. Actually, one might remark that the Catholic Church would do itself a huge favour by ordaining women, because then, as is the case with the male clergy, women would be controlled and subject to obedience and just as fearful as their ordained brothers.

So where *do* women fit in this male-dominant Church with its male-metaphored God? For most people, the metaphors have become literalised, and for them, God is a man, the whole divine reality is male, and this, for most, is essential because of the actual maleness of the human Jesus. This unrelenting male metaphorical language pervades every aspect of Christian life, from history to spirituality, from liturgy to theology, and in the Roman Catholic Church, it persists in the actual patriarchal hierarchy of its ministry and leadership. The theology that is taught in our seminaries and colleges is male theology, even though it occasionally assumes a kind of generic, neutral tone which can mask its real origins in the lives and spiritualities of men. Liturgy too, can adopt a kind of pseudo-inclusive quality, if only in the usual majority of women participants, but even a simple attempt to recognise the presence of women linguistically can provoke outrage. And as the 'new' liturgical texts indicate, the liturgical presence of women is reduced even more, as the texts return to the sixteenth century for their inspiration, symbolic structure and language. The fairly obvious attempt to replace the documents of Vatican II with the *Catechism of the Catholic Church* as the main text for the new evangelisation makes the language more exclusively male. One might be tempted to say, 'Relax, women of the church, this Catechism and this evangelisation are not addressed to you.'

In Advent 2012, a two-part series on RTÉ television explored some aspects of the Irish Church in these first few decades of the twenty-first century. There seemed to be a particular focus on women and one group of women was shown leading their own prayer service as a substitute for an absent priest. These women were conscious participants and spoke easily of ministry and lay participation. They were not just 'filling in'. A later conversation with Diarmuid Martin, the Archbishop of Dublin, seemed to discuss this situation and explore it further as perhaps a sign for the future. The Archbishop's first comment was, 'But we are a hierarchy.' As a woman intensely interested in the history of women in Christianity, I am not unaware of the hierarchical structure of the Church, but this easy personalising of this structure and the consequent confining of women to a permanent secondary place took my breath away. It was a blatant claim. 'We ordained men are in charge and nothing that women do can help the church or alter its structure.' There was no attempt at spin, none of the usual talk about the People of God in the documents of Vatican II, no attempt to recognise the dire situation of the Irish Church under its present leadership. No, there was just a plain statement of what the Church is and was and will be, all worthy of a medieval prince bishop. From the Archbishop's perspective, the hierarchy was the Church and the Church was the hierarchy, and a patriarchal hierarchy at that.

From that hierarchical perspective, the Catholic Church in Ireland and elsewhere is a graded society, where some few people are permanently more important than the vast majority of the members, and these few men are permanently more important than all the women. This male patriarchal hierarchy requires a male God figure. Women have simply no contribution to make. Nothing is asked or expected of them beyond obedience and the acceptance of their lot at the bottom of the patriarchal hierarchy. It is not from any actions of women that the healing of the Church will come. In fact, as always in history, such actions of women will be seen as an unwarranted intrusion on male territory, and this applies to all women without exception, and also to those members of the clergy who choose to recognise the strange anomaly of a woman-free church. Most men also find themselves on the lower rungs of this patriarchal hierarchy, but men at least have grown up with a language and metaphorical system that affirms their existence. Men are not the elephant in the Church.

This is not just the thinking of the hierarchy, but of the vast majority of Catholic clergy and Catholic people, even those who are sympathetic to the 'cause of women'. There have been many attempts to delineate a positive solution to the present Church crisis written by men of impeccable scholarship and great good will. But, almost without exception, these discourses reserve for the last paragraph any mention of women: 'And of course, women ...' The discussion usually ends with a vague and often veiled reference to the priestly ordination of women, or even to the possibility that women might be admitted to the hierarchy as deacons or even cardinals. Given the quasi-infallible state of the church's teaching on the ordination of women, it is often seen as hazardous to speak openly about this subject, and priests who do suffer the consequences.

Ordination, however, is not the answer for women. It has absolutely nothing to do with the current situation which reaches far back into the teaching of Christian anthropology. Women cannot be admitted to a priesthood which is a male construct. The priesthood, as we know it, was designed by men, inhabited by men, theologised by men, liturgised by men and experienced by men. It was designed by men, for men. As such it has produced men of great holiness and brilliant pastoral awareness, as well as men who were profligate and utterly unworthy of the positions they occupied.

The situation of contemporary women in a patriarchal hierarchy is completely anomalous. Later chapters will explore the levels of exclusion developed through history in order to keep women in their place at the bottom, but for the moment it is sufficient to say that women are left to live lives of complete ambiguity in the Church. Every document, every biblical text, every liturgical rubric, every Papal and Episcopal pronouncement, every word from the hierarchy leaves women wondering whether or not they are included. Usually they are not, and if they are, it is usually by a kind of generic implication.

So what are women to do? Sandra Schneiders, professor emerita in the Jesuit School of Theology at the Graduate Theological Union in Berkeley, California, once pointed out that the opening words of the American Constitution, 'All men are created equal ...' included, at the time they were written, only white propertied males. All women and all people of colour and all the poor were explicitly excluded and deemed not to be full human persons. Nevertheless, she remarks, this document gave rise to a thirst for equality as those excluded ones seized the notion and grew to believe that they should be included. Thus the notion of equality expanded gradually to include more and more people in the 'land of the free'. A similar but not identical situation arises within the Christian church. The Good News has been heard at all levels of the male hierarchical structure. It has enriched and liberated people of all classes, women and men, and opened imaginations to the endless possibilities of freedom before God, following the call of Jesus. The Good News has not led to an expansion of the patriarchy. It has not led to inclusion. It has not led to a respect for the contribution of the poor. Women are still the permanently silenced members of the Roman Catholic Church, nothing they think or say is of interest when it comes to formulating teaching, or revising the public prayer of the Church. But the Good News has penetrated the imaginations of people, and the open horizons offered by Jesus continue to inspire people to move beyond the imposed spiritual and theological restrictions.

This reflection applies entirely to the Roman Catholic Church. It is the church of my childhood, and the Church of my present marginal – by patriarchal intent – participation. In following chapters I will try to outline some of the steps that women have taken to survive in this institution, and some of the riches they have experienced, as an inheritance from the community of the early women followers of Jesus, as disciples and apostles.

I have not as yet mentioned power. Power in a patriarchal hierarchy is inevitably used abusively, because it is, by definition, impossible to treat people as equals. The sexual abuse crisis in the Irish Church (and worldwide), showed one particularly horrific face of the abuse of power, but this horror grew out of a context of hierarchical entitlement and privilege that, in every act, only endorsed such apparent privilege. There seems to be little hope of renewal in such a context, because the general context still pertains. Papal writings, especially of the two previous popes, have exhorted to interpersonal love at the expense of institutional justice. Seminaries are being corralled into clerical compounds, where outside influence is kept at bay. A new kind of siege mentality is emerging where, under the guise of the year of faith, some Catholics are being invited to become card-carrying members (*The Tablet*, 25 February 2012). There is much new talk of repentance and atonement and liturgical invitations to present oneself as 'grievously sinful', all directed at the innocent and unprivileged laity. This is surely not Good News, and as we shall see in later chapters, is a particularly male preoccupation.

The recent very low-key commemoration of the fiftieth anniversary of the opening of the Second Vatican Council sends a clear message that, despite theological analyses and conciliar reminiscences, the impetus to renewal is not going to come from a reinvigorated reception of the Council. Indeed, every effort in that direction is diluted by traditionalist interpretations of conciliar teaching, in the interests of 'a hermeneutic of continuity'. During the mid-sixties, when Vatican II was under way, I was somewhat unknowingly engaged in one of the Council's great sources of inspiration – the earliest biblical and patristic years of Christianity. This endeavour came to be called *ressourcement*. I was expanding my studies of our biblical and patristic past to include our matristic heritage, a fairly new endeavour at the time, with little to go on by way of sources. I was seeking, for both personal and professional reasons, some insight into our past as women and the developing attitudes of the Christian Church towards women. The Christian Feminist movement was also beginning to surface, with its new questions and challenges to the tradition. It was, as I remember, an exhilarating time. None of that exhilaration marks this current anniversary, but there is an all-pervading sense of anxiety, darkness, threat and fear, not to mention bewilderment and confusion.

The insights I gained then, not on attitudes towards women by men, but on the women's own understanding and experience of Christianity, will form the substance of the following chapters. It is a largely untold story, and the male-dominated Catholic Church manifests no interest whatsoever in these women and their theology. Nevertheless, the lives and teaching of women throughout the whole span of Christianity seem to offer the only possible alternative to our present waffling. There can no longer be any such thing as a woman-free renewal. I am writing this in the hope that, as women and men Christians, our joint insights, historical and contemporary, may help to renew the church we love.

Catholic Woman/Woman Catholic

There are not many signs to indicate that the Roman Catholic Church, with its patriarchal hierarchy, is capable of, or even desirous of, bringing about an inclusive Christian community after the model of Galatians 3:27–28:

> As many of you as were baptised into Christ have clothed yourselves with Christ. There is no longer Jew or Greek, there is no longer slave or free, there is no longer male and female; for all of you are one in Christ Jesus.

Even Pope Francis, with his refreshing new openness to new possibilities, has definitely linked himself with his predecessors on the subject of women, at least on the subject of women's ordination. When he speaks of a new theology of women, he is definitely not speaking about Christian Feminist theology, but about a theology of women done by men, as it has always been done.

There is, however, an alternative tradition that we can call on. And this is the history of Christian women, who, from the very beginning have been followers of Jesus. However, from approximately the year 55 CE, in the writings of Paul to the Corinthians (of which there will be much more later), women have been silenced and considered of little or no account in the Christian community. Nothing has ever been expected from women except obedience – even up to the present day, as the words of Archbishop Martin indicated (see p. 8). If women are going to participate more fully in the Christian community, it is only on the whim of the male clergy. Nothing is needed from women in terms of female theology or liturgical leadership. In one of the most recent papal allocutions given at the close of the recent Synod of Bishops, women are again confined to the home, where indeed, it is implied, their efforts at the new evangelisation are sorely needed. But this is to emphasise, yet again, the private nature of women's Christian lives. This is the distinction I make between being a Catholic Woman leading a private, non-participatory Christian life, and a Woman Catholic, who brings the whole of her bodily being to her faith, and worships the God in whose image she is made, as a woman.

Catholic women are prescribed to lead private lives, mostly as mothers, and to keep their faith to themselves. The Church seems to have no need of this faith. As far as the institutional Church is concerned, little has changed since Paul's Corinthian letter in 55 CE. Women are to be silent in the churches, subject to their husbands from whom they learn all they need to know. Not only is it unlawful for women to speak in church, it is shameful; that is, such behaviour would go against their very nature. It would fly in the face of everything that God has intended for the female of the species. This is the back drop to all Papal and Episcopal pronouncements about women. The Church is a hierarchical patriarchy, a graded society where women are placed on the very lowest rung.

The interpretation of Paul's Letter to the Corinthians was questioned by Pope Paul VI in the late sixties, shortly after the close of Vatican II. He requested the Pontifical Biblical Commission to examine the text to see what it might really mean. He offered two possible choices, which offer a quite unique insight into the New Testament exegesis of the time. The first possibility was that this text was indeed the Word of God, inerrant and true for all time and in all places, and therefore impossible to change. The second possibility was that this text represented a pastoral decision made by Paul in a particular place, Corinth, and at a particular time, the middle of the first century of Christianity. If this were so, then the teaching could be changed in another pastoral decision in another place and at another time. The Pontifical Biblical Commission opted for the latter solution. Apart from all the questions this particular decision raises for those who tend to read the Scriptures literally and see the Word of God contained *verbatim* in each word of the text, it gave Paul VI the opportunity to declare publicly that the Church now believed that women's silencing and invisibility were at an end. The possibility that the Church could now begin to harness the gifts and energies and wisdom of women presented itself.

This is not however, what happened. Pope Paul chose to make a symbolic gesture, which in fact was missed by most of the Church. Perhaps that was precisely the intention, since symbolic gestures, by their very nature, are easily ignored or misinterpreted. What Pope Paul VI chose to do in 1970 was to make Catherine of Siena and Teresa of Avila Doctors of the Church, Catherine representing all lay women, and Teresa representing all consecrated religious women. The occasion, important though it was, barely caused a ripple, and the consequences, in terms of the intentionality of the act, have been almost negligible. Since then Thérèse of Lisieux (1997) and Hildegarde of Bingen (2012) have been made Doctors of the Church with similarly negligible consequences for Catholic women and even for many women Catholics. The intention surely was to announce to the Church that the writings of these women had been recognised as of similar importance to the Church as the writings of the male Doctors, but no analysis of this situation has become general, and the writings of the four women Doctors remain practically unknown. The one exception might be Thérèse of Lisieux, but it is usually not her Doctorate for which she is remembered, but her 'Little Way'.

It is within the possibilities offered by Pope Paul VI to the Pontifical Biblical Commission in the late 1960s that the characteristics of Catholic Women and Women Catholics are clearly and definitively delineated. Catholic Women, it is believed, are placed by God in a particular position of silence and invisibility, obedient to men and at their bidding and service. They are the ones who are taught, and they are never to be seen as official teachers, especially as teachers of men.

Women are the listeners, the taught, the silent unquestioning ones, and even though the vast majority of Catholic women would probably reject this designation, this is precisely the basic ecclesial premise of their lives. It is also the basic ecclesial practice of the Church of our day, including the Church in Ireland. Women have no official role in the Church, except occasionally, on the whim of men, to fill in gaps, that would always be better filled by any available man. Women study men's theology – the theology of the new women doctors of the Church has never become integrated with 'mainstream' theology. Women often have spoken and unspoken misgivings about this state of affairs, but it is universally believed that there is just 'theology', a kind of pseudo-generic phenomenon, created by men for men in the words of men, and altered hardly at all by the presence of women students. *The Catechism of the Catholic Church* is a brilliant example of this wholly-male theology, and according to the most recent Synod of Bishops, it is to be the main instrument of teaching for the Year of Faith (2012–13), and the New Evangelisation, in preference, it seems, both to the Bible and the official documents of Vatican II. The language of the Catechism is so male-centred that it is often unintentionally humorous. Whether Catholic Women notice this or not, Women Catholics (whom we shall describe for much of the remainder of this book) find it almost impossible to read or take seriously. They are not addressed, their lives are not considered, and they are subsumed under the male persona.

I am using the term 'Catholic Women' to include all those who apparently find this situation to be quite normal, impossible to change, and relatively tolerable. 'Apparently' is the important word in the above sentence, for even if such Catholic women have questions about this situation, they keep their questions to themselves because they see no possible alternative to the current situation. They often focus on the personality of the local priest or bishop, his kindness, pastoral concern or good homilies. The larger ecclesial situation remains beyond their concern.

This book is designed to illustrate that there is an alternative to the current male-dominant situation, and that there has always been an alternative. There is a genuine, legitimate, and continuous tradition of Christianity as experienced, celebrated, and interpreted by women. Even the teaching of the four women Doctors of the Church has been treated as almost an irrelevancy, and their doctorates are seen as honours rather than as a distinct contribution to the theology and meaning of Christianity. It is the thesis of this book that unless attention is paid to women's contribution to Christianity, then Christianity will practically disappear. The fading of what can be called 'men's church' is already well under way.

Before delineating the Women Christian and Catholic tradition, it is important to try to spell out where the theory and theology of the Catholic Woman tradition comes from. It is a long and quite consistent story of women's silencing. Nuanced somewhat through the ages, but easily concealed in the phrases of recent popes about the 'special nature of women', or even the 'particular genius' of women. It is apparently a theory and theology accepted by all clergy and the vast majority of Catholics without a second thought.

This long story can be divided for convenience into four phases, the first three being sometimes chronological, and sometimes coexisting all at the same time. For most of recent and ancient history, it was accepted without question that women were inferior to men in every way: physically, intellectually and, especially, in the skills of leadership and decision-making. The reasons for this have to do partly with ignorance about the nature of human reproduction, where the male was seen as the sole generating force, and women were seen merely as the location of the process. The discovery of the female ovum in recent centuries changed this perception in practical terms, but by then attitudes and relationships and theologies had been worked out in a totally patriarchal context. In pre-Christian times, Aristotle was the main articulator of this view, and, in the context of medieval scholasticism, Thomas Aquinas repeated the 'wisdom' of Aristotle almost verbatim, namely that woman was a *mas occasionatus*, an accidental man. The male was the 'normative' human being, the one who needed no explanation, and the one who could then prescribe the realities of her life to the woman, his natural inferior. Women could contribute nothing to the phenomenon of humanity, except to live as 'nature' and men dictated.

In Christian times this situation was seen – and still is – as the 'will of God'. The life and teaching of Jesus of Nazareth offers a direct challenge to this understanding of humanity as female and male; as early as twenty years after the death of Jesus in the teaching of Paul, the challenges of Jesus had been subsumed by the traditional practices of society. The women of the Gospel, however, stand out as the perpetual biblical challenge to the male interpretation, as we shall see in Chapter Two. The Gospel women are our dangerous memory.

It was an insight of Augustine of Hippo (354–430) that contested this understanding to some extent. It seemed to him that if God had created women in 'his image' then it would not be right to call women inferior. His version of the situation of women has come to be called by Pope John Paul II, 'ontological complementarity', which means, apparently, that women and men are designed by God to fill prescribed roles, that the male is the normatively human, but by fitting into a lesser status, women can attain the status of a quasi-human. It is this understanding that has led to the insistence, in Vatican documents, that the language of the Church always be male, to represent the real humanity of men. Women are subsumed within this and do not need to be mentioned separately. What men do is 'normal' and sufficient. In the ecclesiastical context, these prescribed roles of women and men have continued relatively unaltered down through the centuries to our own day. These roles take their origin in the physical shape and purpose of female and male bodies, roles that have been socially and religiously articulated as 'femininity' and 'masculinity'. Women are designed by nature – and God – to function mostly in the private sphere in silence, service, and obedience, and in their particular 'genius' of nurturing. Men are designed for the public arena as rulers, thinkers, teachers, masters and decision-makers. In this dualistic world of strength and weakness, ruling and obeying, men always appear on the positive side of the dualism and women on the negative.

The first theological articulation of the reasons for women's silence and confinement to the private sphere comes in the First Letter to Timothy, Chapter 2, vv. 11–15:

> Let a woman learn in silence with full submission. I permit no woman to teach or to have authority over a man; she is to keep silent. For Adam was formed first, then Eve; and Adam was not deceived, but the woman was deceived and became a transgressor. Yet she will be saved through childbearing.

This has always been seen as the Biblical explanation as to why women have to take the second place, humanly speaking, and why they are not really seen as fully human. This theological explanation of the position of women in God's plan became a kind of mantra and was repeated constantly and consistently throughout history – women were 'created second and sinned first'. From this all manner of conclusions were drawn and still continue to be drawn in papal writing explicitly, and in most other ecclesiastical writing by implication.

One of the relatively recent extrapolations on this passage comes in the writing of Pope Pius XII in 1941. The pope was speaking to a group of newly-weds that year and his words are among the best examples of the workings of the theory of complementarity. I shall just refer to his three initial points.

The pope welcomes the young couples and reminds them that they have taken their marriage vows with 'solemn and free consent' as between 'persons absolutely equal'. But this is not the whole story and as he continues we see a wonderful example of how the Church can say two entirely contradictory things about women at the same time. The pope reminds them that 'in that same moment you founded a society', the family, which has a head, and whose 'power of headship' comes from God alone. Therefore, in this family, the husband acts as head in everything with God's authority, exercising this authority over his wife, who has been 'given' to him to form this family.

The pope now moves to the Hebrew Scriptures and the Second Creation account, the story of Adam and Eve. The authority of the husband is similar to and based on the authority of Adam over Eve. He then repeats the lines of Timothy, which we have quoted above, pointing out that Adam was created first and that Eve sinned first. And this sin of Eve, rooted in curiosity, brought havoc to the whole human race, and still does.

The pope's third initial point has to do with baptism, where 'both spouses were equally and immediately united to Christ', and he quotes the relevant passage in Paul's Letter to the Galatians (3:26–28). Here also, quite astonishingly, but quite logically, the negative comes quickly. This equality, the pope teaches, does not apply to women in either the family or the Church, since these are visible public societies, and women must, of necessity, remain invisible and exist only in the private and obedient sphere of the home.

The astonishing thing is how easily the pope says two entirely contradictory things at the same time – women are absolutely equal, but also inferior; women are equally created by God, but secondarily and sinfully; and women are absolutely and equally united to Christ in baptism, but not really since they are subordinate to men. This is the theory of complementarity at work. This is also one of the main reasons for priestly celibacy, since the male cleric must be preserved from the sinful female. It is obvious that, even though not expressed as such, this is the main and definitive reason against the ordination of women to the priesthood. The exclusion of women from priesthood is so great that it cannot even be discussed.

In this church which still functions explicitly in the sphere of 'ontological complementarity', women are not seen to have full human qualities, and certainly not the qualities of leadership, intellect, decision-making and teaching that are necessary for ordination. No more elaborate explanation need be sought as the Bishop of Meath recently (20 January 2013) said in a television interview on the subject of women, 'This will not happen.' The silencing and even excommunication of clergy who espouse the cause of women are by now, sadly, too numerous to mention.

With the exception of a brief period in the fourth century (Chapter Three), when it was taught that after the renunciation of sex women and men were equal, ontological complementarity has remained the official teaching of the Catholic Church for millennia. This teaching has also vastly influenced the inner life of most other churches, even of those who ordain women. There have been occasional nuances, and the teaching is sometimes not as blatant as it once was, but the position remains the same. In the world that is unceasingly called 'secular', and is usually described as 'assaulting' the Church, many women and men have moved on to a fuller understanding of the nature of humanity as female and male.

During the last part of the twentieth century, then, a new understanding of the relationship between women and men has been emerging. It has been called mutuality, and gives equal voice and equal ear to both women and men. Within the Catholic Church, the voice of women is never heard. All is prescribed for women by men. There is not the slightest interest in what women think about anything, even the most intimate issues of their lives. Mutuality is a recognition that women and men come to a relationship, or exist as separate beings on their own terms. It moves beyond the strictures of femininity and masculinity. It recognises that women and men are interdependent and that the voice of women and the experience of women is just as essential to this situation as the voice of men. Mutuality is a move beyond stereotypes and a discovery of the unique gifts of each person. This is where the Woman Catholic exists, knowing that her femaleness, her womanhood, cannot be predetermined by men, ordained or otherwise. It is this Woman Catholic who will occupy our attention primarily in the remaining chapters. Even though, throughout the history of Christianity, Woman Christians/Catholics have been seen as an intrusion on the Church of men, and have been treated as such, there is a long, continuous history of women believers who thought for themselves and imaged God for themselves and taught this to others. Four of them have been named as Doctors of the Church, as we have seen. This is a legitimate chapter in Christian history which has been utterly ignored by the male theologians and clergy of all ages, including our own.

The Woman Catholic is a self-defined woman who fully accepts her female nature and the Christian teaching that she, as female, is made in the image of God. This God, then, cannot be an exclusively male-metaphored God. The fact of femaleness is the starting point, and for most Women Catholics, it is a starting point of grace, not of original sinfulness. 'Just to be born is grace enough,' they profess, and 'my real me is God,' as the mystic Catherine of Genoa proclaimed. This sets up a completely new theological agenda, starting from the lives of women and their God, as reflected on by women.

The difficulty lies in the fact that the history of women in Christianity is largely unknown. It has been erased from the consciousness of male historians, male theologians and male clergy, from pope to parish priest. Nevertheless, it is possible to trace a continuous history of Women Christians from the very first days of the Gospel story. With the exception of the Women Mystics of the Middle Ages, these women have left little trace of their lives, and certainly nothing of their voices. Nevertheless, it is possible to trace their presence, as endless Synods, Episcopal and Papal pronouncements, and theological and saintly denunciations of the activities of women litter the pages of Church history. Male historians unceasingly write of the 'intrusions' of women on the 'normal' male life of the Church. They are speaking of women emerging from their imposed private sphere on to the public stage, and usurping the roles of men. It is these women who will be the centre of our attention.

The starting point will be, of course, the biblical women and the women followers of Jesus of Nazareth. These women were the women who earned Paul's strictures about their teaching. Jesus might have welcomed them – and he did – but Paul was not going to do likewise. We will turn next to the fourth- and fifth-century women who invented urban monasticism for women, a form of religious life for women that brought the 'Fathers' of the Church rushing in to regulate it on male terms. The quasi-episcopal abbesses, with their glorious self-confidence will conclude this section.

The magnificent women mystics of the Middle Ages (1150–1450) will take up three chapters as we follow their teachings from Doctor Hildegarde of Bingen to Doctor Teresa of Avila. The explosion of women missionaries after the Council of Trent, which had practically ignored women completely, will be almost familiar to people who grew up in the Catholic Church from the twenties on. It is a story that is coming to an end in our lifetime. The Marian centuries bring the story to our own time, or at least up to the 1950s.

For women, the Second Vatican Council was, for the most part, a repetition of the ancient prescriptions, but as always, when a door is opened, women rush through. This time, against all the odds, it was the door of Women's ministry. As a result, the face of the church, though not its teaching, was changed dramatically. As well as this, the promotion of biblical scholarship and biblical spirituality by the Council awakened in women a need to participate in their own traditions and spirituality that has not been, nor can it be, quenched.

Around the same time as the Second Vatican Council, that is the mid-sixties, the arrival of Christian Feminism brought a whole new sense of liberation, at least to some Women Catholics. Feminism vastly disturbed the Catholic Women, that is most women in the Catholic Church, and this breach has never been healed. Christian Feminism opened doors to women theologians, exegetes and other scholars to begin a female-based exploration of the traditional documents of the Church. The official church, at every level, fears this development and denounces it at every opportunity.

The conclusion will look to the future of the Catholic Church and suggest that the long, continuous, brilliant and radical history of women's Christian presence may break the deadlock of a Church which seems to be stuck in its own intransigence.

Women and Scripture

Among the most explosive words in the New Testament, in view of subsequent historical developments in the Christian Church, are the words that come towards the very end of Mark's Gospel (15:40-41): 'And there were women there …' As we shall see, these brief words establish women as apostles, disciples and the only witnesses of the foundational events of Christianity. Why explosive? Because these five words cancel out the whole Christian male structure built on male only apostles, male only priests, and male only teachers. Certainly there must have been other bystanders at this murderous event, but they were not accounted as witnesses. As recently as 31 January 2012, the 'Pope's theologian' is still repeating the 'male-only' dictum, and still rooting it on false premises. The tragedy now is that he is using it to justify the Catholic Church's treatment of several priests on several continents for daring to raise the question of women priests.

Mark's Gospel, written some forty years after the death of Jesus, is recognised as probably the most historical of the four gospels. As we read through this gospel, there is no hint that there are women disciples among the group of those 'following' Jesus. The 'following of Jesus' is Mark's technical term for discipleship. There are important vignettes about women who were healed by Jesus, but there is simply no mention of women disciples. It is only when Mark has announced the total failure and flight of the male apostles and disciples in Chapter Fourteen, v. 50, that it becomes necessary for him to bring the women disciples to the fore, to name their leaders, state that they had 'followed'

Jesus from Galilee, and were there at the crucial last moments of the life of Jesus:

> There were also women there looking on from a distance; among them were Mary Magdalene, and Mary the mother of James the Younger and of Joses, and Salome. These used to follow him and provide for him when he was in Galilee; and there were many other women who had come up with him to Jerusalem.

All four gospels go on to testify that the women were also the first witnesses of the Resurrection. It is apparent all through the Gospel of Mark that Jesus was not the kind of leader the men wanted or expected, but that the women seemed to have understood the fatal consequences of the teaching of Jesus and remained faithful in spite of the tragedy of the Crucifixion.

Whenever the male apostles and disciples are mentioned, Peter is always named as their leader. Whenever the female apostles and disciples are mentioned, Mary of Magdala is named as their leader. Her companions in Mark are Mary the mother of James the Younger and Joses, and Salome and 'many other women'. It is appropriate then to envisage that these women were present from the beginning of the ministry of Jesus and to re-read the whole Gospel knowing that, though unmentioned, Mary of Magdala and the women were present. Mark seems to set the pattern for the vast majority of other Christian writers, who also fail to mention the presence of women in Christian history. We have come to know, through Christian texts, that it is quite possible, down to the most recent scholarly tomes, to write a critically lauded history of Christianity without ever mentioning women as integral participants, or even as minimally part of the story.

Does scripture, then, ever include women as full and active members of the religious community? Scholars have identified a few passages that are radical and revelatory in their full inclusion of women and men as equal partners in the religious project that is Christianity. Here we will just look at four of these texts: the First Creation Story, the *acta et verba Jesus*, the Pentecost Story, and the Baptismal Hymn quoted

14

by Paul in Galatians. As we shall see, these texts remain as a continuous challenge and rebuke to the Christian community down through the generations for its arrogant dismissal of so many groupings of human beings because of their colour, creed, sexual identity or sexual preference, or indeed because of their poverty or lack of social status.

The First Creation Story
This is not the place, nor do I have the expertise, to provide an exhaustive exegesis of the First Creation Story: 'So God created humankind in his image, in the image of God he created them, male and female he created them' (Gen 1:27). It is enough to point out that these extraordinary words on the first page of the book of Genesis reach out a hand of inclusion to all women and men with the assurance that they are part of the same human family, equally created in the image of God. It would hardly be an exaggeration to say that almost every other word of scripture contradicts this message. These words were written at a time, several hundred years before the Christian era, when the natural inferiority of women was taken for granted. Despite myths of Amazon women and female goddesses, it seems that for most of human history, women were seen as inferior in every way to men. The Greek philosopher Aristotle, repeated hundreds of years later by the Catholic theologian Thomas Aquinas, deemed that women were *mas occasionatus*, accidental men. It was a long-standing male-normative view of humanity. The natural human was the male, females were the result of an accident.

This view of women is still deeply entrenched in our minds as women and men of the twenty-first century, though its articulation is less blatant, except perhaps in Vatican documents. For a brief moment in the fourth and fifth centuries, women and men were seen as potential equals when sex was removed from the equation, as we shall see in the next chapter. It was probably Augustine of Hippo, however, who provided Western culture, particularly the Catholic Church, with the standard understanding of the relationship of women and men which still dominates Catholic teaching, and still lies at the root of such teachings as the ban on the ordination of women and the celibacy of the clergy, to name but the two most controversial at the moment. Augustine suggested that after reading the First Creation Story it was not appropriate to say that women were inferior to men but that they were in a state of complementarity with men (called ontological complementarity by Pope John Paul II). This meant, as has been exhaustingly catalogued by most recent popes, that women and men had different gifts and different roles to play in the great human dance of existence. Unfortunately for women, their roles fell on the inferior side of the scale, while the roles of men were the well-recognised ones of leadership, teaching, authority in the family and, of course, religious leadership. The major conclusion was that men belonged to the public sphere and women to the private sphere. This was the articulation of millennia of men. Women were never consulted on what might be their version of this complementarity. In other words, it was a prescribed complementarity, because it was ontological. It is amazing, and often quite amusing, how generation after generation of religious leaders repeated these strictures in order to exclude women from citizenship and the right to vote, not to mention ordination or any public religious role.

The revelation of the created human equality of the female and the male, then, has rarely been used as a basis for theological thought in the Catholic Church. Theology rarely draws attention to women at all, except with regard to their danger to men. Catholic theology has always been based on total sexual differentiation. In official theological anthropology, it is still not entirely clear whether the Catholic Church teaches that there are one or two human natures, that is one shared human nature or two based on sexual differentiation.

This theology of sexual differentiation is still the official teaching of the Roman Catholic Church, and, as we have seen, underlies much of their intransigence about women. Because society no longer distinguishes prescribed spheres for women and men in the Western world, the Church has had to alter its approach somewhat, but it is just a question of coming up with more and more articulations of why nothing has really changed, and more nuanced explanations of the same old theology.

With the arrival of the feminist movement in the middle of the twentieth century, and the retrieval of women's voices, several new anthropologies have been articulated by women philosophers, theologians, sociologists and psychologists. A new form of relationship has been described as 'mutuality'. This is a relationship beyond imposed stereotypes of complementarity or masculinity and femininity, where women and men really do face one another on a perfectly equal footing. For many women in the twenty-first century, this is the way they live their lives. They know that there is a complementarity between women and men, but not an imposed form of relationship. Each person, female or male, brings the whole of themselves to a relationship, not previously specified bits of themselves. Mutuality is still a journey for most human beings, but it is a journey of discovery and joy, not an imposed punishment for Eve's sin.

We should never forget, however, the power of imposed models of sexual differentiation, whether Eve comes into the equation or not. The history of spousal abuse lies here as well as the history of clerical child abuse. Human beings, female and male, find the notions of equal regard and equal respect very difficult. Respect for the human body, female and male, seems to be lessening, with growing forms of poverty, violence and torture. The First Creation Story has returned to centre stage in the writings of ecologists and feminists, but the implications of human equality, of women and men equally created in the image of a God, who must then be imaged as female as well as male, has made very little headway in the theology of the Catholic Church, or indeed of most Christian churches.

Acta et verba Jesus

The four gospels, despite their frequent blindness to, silencing and diminishing of women, still offer us an extraordinary example of the discipleship of equals in the words and deeds of Jesus. He stands out from his contemporaries like a glorious ray of sunshine in his respect for and ability to relate to women without a trace of condescension. It is not only his dealings with the individual women that he meets but also the very core of the gospel he preaches. Once heard, this is a gospel that gnaws at the heart and challenges all human beings to recognise that the first are the last, and the most negligible are first; that it is the widow who gives her last farthing that gives the most, not the ostentatious rich; that the humble will be exalted and that the mighty will be cast down and the lowly be raised up. This leveling of human and social injustice is at the heart of the message of Jesus and has, over the centuries, called women to move beyond the patriarchal and hierarchical restrictions on their lives. Sometimes these restrictions are obvious and oppressive and violent, but sometimes they are phrased in more deceptive language about the peculiar and beautiful genius of women. Women have learned well over the centuries that when they are called 'special' by Catholic clergy of whatever rank, that it is just the gateway to another restriction.

Such speech never came from the lips of Jesus, as remembered and recorded in the gospels. He seems to be able to meet women as equals and to recognise that their faith in him and his message is unique. Whether it is the Syrophoenician woman in Mark (7:24–37), from whom he learned that his mission could not be restricted to his own people, or the woman of Samaria in John (4:1–42), for whom he ignored the rules about Jewish men addressing strange women, or the bent woman in Luke (13:10–17), for whom he broke the Sabbath laws, Jesus is remembered as treating women with the utmost respect and sensitivity.

It is true that there is no recorded instance of Jesus calling women to be his apostles, nor does a woman's name appear among the 'Twelve', but we know that the very process of the writing and 'canonisation' of the gospels deliberately excluded all traces of the leadership of women. What is clear is that the women disciples took the initiative to follow Jesus, as women have done down through the centuries, even when they were being accused of intruding on male territory. It is also obvious that the process of reducing women's dignity and role, and confining them to the house, as was the practice in the ancient world, is already at work in the gospels. Luke, for example, never calls women 'disciples', but interprets their presence as wealthy benefactors as, for example, in Luke 8:1–3. It is also Luke who set in motion a huge imaginative scenario of fallen, sinful women on their knees before Jesus, washing his feet with tears and drying them with long blond hair (7:36–50). This image, falsely and fictionally, resonates down through the centuries in art, liturgy, poetry – even in the horrific invention of the Magdalene laundries in Ireland, where the fallen woman image got superimposed over the image of Mary of Magdala, the first witness of the Resurrection. There was never a similar imaginative scenario about fallen men, who, as is obvious, were there in equal measure.

There are dozens of other gospel images of women being treated honourably by Jesus, but their evangelical effect and imaginative power have been diminished by centuries of male interpretation, and actual ignorance of the gospels. It is only since the Second Vatican Council that biblical familiarity has become more widespread, but as with most traditions, we see what we want to see.

The Pentecost Story
When one begins to seek out the presence of women in Christian history, the absence of the voice of women, the teaching of women, and the authoritative force of women reflecting on their own gospel-inspired lives, one is faced with utter silence and invisibility. Women are silent in the Churches, and the tradition of silencing women will be explored below. Nevertheless, the Pentecost story (Acts 2:1–4), claimed by generations of male Christian leaders as the source of their authority, was also shared by women, as the passage in Acts clearly portrays. This empowerment of women by the Spirit was erased from the story so thoroughly that even as we read the words describing the

presence of women, 'all these were constantly devoting themselves to prayer, together with certain women, including Mary the mother of Jesus, as well as his brothers' (Acts 1:14). 'All these' presumably refers to the reconstituted and reassembled Twelve, and the 'certain women' refers to the women witnesses, led by Mary of Magdala, who had gathered together the fearful and faithless male apostles to report on the foundational events of the death and resurrection of Jesus. How extraordinary, then, that the women were excluded from the public acknowledgement of their reception of the gifts of the Spirit, together with the men. As the text says, 'they were all filled with the Holy Spirit' (Acts 2:4).

It is to this text that the Catholic Church has always returned to explain and justify male apostolic succession. Countless numbers of confirmation classes have taken place with countless generations of children drawing pictures of twelve men and one woman, Mary the Mother of Jesus, receiving the tongues of fire symbolising the Holy Spirit. The 'certain women' and all the others have been airbrushed out of the picture. It is a vivid example of the 'elephant in the room' of this book's title, this time in the upper room. As is clear from the history of the Church, this continuous male apostolic succession cannot really be verified in all ages, but the perpetual exclusion of women from this empowering gift of spiritual leadership has definitely been obvious in all places and at all times, to the present day.

Baptismal Hymn

As many of you as were baptised into Christ have clothed yourselves with Christ. There is no longer Jew or Greek, there is no longer slave or free, there is no longer male and female; for all of you are one in Christ Jesus. (Galatians 3:27–28)

This is, perhaps, one of the most challenging biblical passages, part of a biblical hymn from the earliest days of Christianity. It obviously describes a vision of community that has never been achieved by the

Church, and, given the teaching about the secondary and neglected place of women in the Church, is never likely to be achieved. As we know, it is not even a goal of the Catholic Church, deserving not even a mention in the programmes of the New Evangelisation for this Year of Faith (2012-13), celebrating the fiftieth anniversary of the Second Vatican Council. The awareness of the evils of slavery and anti-semitism have troubled the consciences of Catholics since the Council, and some efforts have been advanced to remove these evils from the Christian community and the larger society. But the evils of sexism, the preference of male over female, the deliberate patriarchal structure of the Catholic Church, has instead become a mark of orthodoxy. Many men who have spoken out on behalf of women's dignity and women's possible contribution to the church have been sidelined or even excommunicated. This is such an anomalous situation that it is hard to conceptualise it. It is, of course, shrouded in the language of law (we are not permitted), the language of a literalist exegesis (Jesus did not do it), or in the past fifty years or so, the language of a sentimentalised rhetoric about the particular genius of women. On the contrary, Pope Francis has spoken continuously and consistently about inclusion, but several Catholic writers have rushed in to save the Church from the pope's inclusive agenda.

Commentators on the biblical text are well aware that total unity and inclusive community will never be achieved, but this ancient biblical belief challenges all believers to take the current possible steps to move in that direction. Catholics have become sensitised to the presence of many kinds of slavery in their midst – if only recently and sometimes grudgingly, but with the evidence and horror stories from the enslaved women of the Magdalene laundries, a sense of justice has risen up in our communities. It is apparent that there is still a degree of racism at every level in our society, but, since the Second Vatican Council, there is a public discourse about the evils of racism and anti-Semitism. There is no such public discourse about the diminishment of women in the Catholic Church. Indeed it is specifically forbidden. Despite an apparently unending series of papal writings about women, and endless attempts at a literalist revision of biblical and historical data, the argument has proceeded no further than 'we are not allowed'. Most of this discourse, of course, is about the priestly ordination of women in the Catholic Church, but the argumentation forbidding ordination (at the present time in a quasi-infallible state), just serves to shroud in obscurity the general situation. Women have nothing to offer, they have no contribution to make, their voices are not necessary. All that is asked is silence and obedience.

How did this state of affairs happen? From what particular biblical stock has all this arisen? What hymn sheet (to use an over-used current cliché) are they all singing from? It is the biblical account of the Second Creation Story, which has remarkably overshadowed the message of Jesus in so many and such far-reaching ways. The four previous biblical accounts about freedom, dignity, inclusivity, the discipleship of equals, the equal creation of women and men in the image of God and their equal reception of the Holy Spirit, have all been reinterpreted to fit into the main biblical source of traditional Catholic theology – the story of Adam and Eve.

The Second Creation Story, Genesis 2 and 3

Apart from the Creationist world view, which apparently accepts the six days of creation as a literal historical happening, much use has not been made in theology until very recently of the wonderful and expansive world view of the First Creation Story. The Story of Adam and Eve, their origins in the dust of the earth, the 'Original Sin' of Eve, the expulsion from the Garden of Eden, and the subsequent punishments of hard labour both of the soil to produce crops and of procreation to carry on the human race, has powerfully occupied our imaginations. It is ubiquitous in art and literature. Not only that, it provides the main source of much of Catholic theology in its apparent explanation of Redemption, Grace, the Life and Death of Jesus, the understanding of all human beings as sinners and born in sin. It has haunted the theology of the Eucharist as Sacrifice, it has mutilated the notion of divinity, and has peopled hell with all those who did not accept this Christian message. But above all, it has made Eve, and after her all other women, responsible for this state of affairs. We women are daughters of Eve and generations of patristic scholars, scholastic theologians, papal encyclicals, and ordinary homely parish sermons have reminded us of this. It is interesting to look at the next generation of women, who have never internalised these messages and who have, because of Eve, lost interest in a church which is not interested in them.

As we have seen earlier, it is the apostle Paul who first articulates demands that women not take the inclusive message of Jesus as applying to them. He demands silence in 1 Cor 14:34–36:

> As in all the churches of the saints, women should be silent in the churches. For they are not permitted to speak, but should be subordinate, as the law also says. If there is anything they need to know, let them ask their husbands at home. For it is shameful for a woman to speak in church.

It has often been pointed out by scripture scholars that this is probably not from the pen of Paul himself, but a later interpolation. This text, however, has functioned throughout Christian history as if it were Pauline, and with his apostolic authority. It can equally be pointed out that, for many women, this cannot possibly be the Word of God in an inspired essentialist way. As we have seen above, this text bothered Pope Paul VI in the late 1960s and resulted, after consultation with the Pontifical Biblical Commission, in naming this text as not the inspired Word of God, but a pastoral decision made by Paul in Corinth around the year 55 CE. Paul had, apparently, found the message of Jesus too demanding, and lapsed back into the standard cultural and religious practice of his day, which saw women as inferior, subordinate to their male superiors, silent, private and ontologically incapable of any kind of leadership or public authoritative speech. Most people don't comment on how the message of Jesus, the Good News for all, is progressively modified by Paul and his descendants in favour of the religiously and culturally dominant theories of their age, and therefore deliberately excluding women, slaves and eventually all non-white peoples.

In the Letter to the Colossians, also probably deutero-Pauline, an effort is made to Christianise this ancient pagan scheme by tacking on the words 'in the Lord': 'Wives, be subject to your husbands, as is fitting in the Lord. Husbands love your wives and never treat them harshly' (Col 3:18–19).

It is only when we come to the Letters to Timothy, which are definitely deutero-Pauline, however, that this pagan modification of the Christian message is put on a firm theological footing which has lasted in Papal and Episcopal teaching until the present day. It is in these letters that the figure of Eve is introduced as the definitive image of Christian womanhood.

> Let a woman learn in silence with full submission. I permit no woman to teach or to have authority over a man; she is to keep silent. For Adam was formed first, then Eve; and Adam was not deceived, but the woman was deceived and became a transgressor. Yet she will be saved through childbearing. (1 Tim 2:11–15)

This then, became the definitive theological understanding of women: they were created second and sinned first. This phrase rings like a mantra through Christian history and theology, and lies like a lodestone behind all official teaching on women, whether it is politely (more or less) tweaked in the twenty-first century to indicate the impossibility of the priestly ordination of women, or the absolute necessity of priestly celibacy. Since women have never been officially allowed to speak for themselves, this male version, and even celibate male version of who women are has formed the basis of the official understanding of womanhood. As we have seen, this modification of the Good News of liberation and inclusiveness has continued to mark the Church at every level. Generation after generation, it is nuanced, depending on the times and cultures, but no women's voices have ever been officially heard in the Roman Catholic Church, nor in most other churches until very recently.

Silencing women, however, was not seen as sufficient, they also had to be demonised and vilified in the image of their mother, Eve. It is true that Mary, the mother of Jesus, was progressively glorified, in contrast to Eve, from as early as the writings of Justin Martyr and Irenaeus, who were among the earliest of the Western Christian writers in the first and second centuries of Christianity. It was taught that Mary re-wrote the life of Eve in every way, as for example, while Eve listened to the devil, Mary listened to the Angel Gabriel. But Mary was essentially inimitable, especially in the portrayal of her gifts in the first one thousand years. Mary was a virgin mother and as unlike all other women as possible. Mary will be central to the next chapter.

One more scriptural detail has to be added here, although it has functioned as a very great weight in the lives of many women. As we have seen, the Good News of Jesus was progressively modified for many reasons, but perhaps primarily to allay the suspicions of the Roman Empire about this new religious movement. I am conscious that this may be too bland an explanation, in view of the very early male-dominant leadership. As women were returned to the privacy of their homes (theologically speaking, at first), so also were slaves returned to the ownership of their masters and mistresses. As Paul initially teaches in the Letter to Philemon, the slave, Onesimus, is to be treated 'like my own child'. He is no longer slave, but a Christian and a brother. Paul, from prison, sends him back to his former owner. When many slave owners had become part of the Christian community, however, this message is again modified in the post-Pauline literature, this time in the first Letter of Peter, which is, of course, also post-Petrine. It is astonishing how quickly the Good News becomes bad news for women, slaves and so many others. This instruction of 'Peter' lets us into the fairly vicious world of the Roman Empire and a new theology of suffering which is one of the most toxic parts of our Christian inheritance.

Slaves, accept the authority of your masters, with all deference, not only those who are kind and gentle, but even those who are harsh. For it is a credit to you if, being aware of God, you endure pain while suffering unjustly … In the same way, wives accept the authority of your husbands. (1 Pet 2:18–20; 3:1)

This sinister teaching shows just how much the Christian Church has modified the Good News. As a woman or slave, it sends shivers down one's spine. The burden of the Christian teaching of love is now placed firmly on the shoulders of the weakest members of the Christian community. Those who are dominated by masters and husbands are instructed to bear abuse and harshness gladly, to 'be aware of God', and to remember that Jesus suffered also without complaint. What makes this teaching so vicious is that there never follows an instruction to the masters and husbands to modify their behaviour and to imitate the actions and message of Jesus. A similar message was contained in the speech of Pope Paul VI at the end of the Second Vatican Council when he instructed women, familiar with cradles and graves, to 'hold back the hand of men lest they destroy the world'. Nowhere in his speech was there a similar exhortation to men to stop the behaviours that would lead to world destruction.

I need now to return briefly to the two women whose names are most familiar to Christians from the biblical tradition – that is, apart from Eve. I am speaking of Mary, the mother of Jesus and Mary of Magdala. As I said, Mary will be central to the next chapter. Here, it is only necessary to point out how unjust the Christian teachers have been in their emphasis only on the virginity of Mary. Mary appears in the biblical story under two other guises – disciple and prophet. The Gospel of Luke paints Mary as the model of disciples as she complies with the word of God, as, for example, in the Visitation scene (1, 39–56), and in so many other scenes and parables. It is obvious that he is nuancing the rather harsher picture of Mark with regard to Mary's discipleship, but this image has not taken up residence in the Christian imagination, as the virgin image has.

Even less has the image of Mary as prophet, even though the Magnificat from the same first chapter of Luke has become part of the daily prayer of the Church. The words have become so familiar that we have failed to see their power. Mary sings about the destruction of unjust power and the abolition of social structures that only serve to leave people hungry and destitute. It is a powerful message of justice that was named by Martin Luther as the essential daily prayer of everyone in a position of power.

We now return briefly to Mary of Magdala. Dozens of books, scholarly and fictional, have appeared recently about the life of this extraordinary woman, about whom we know so little. It is obvious from the biblical testimony that Mary was the leader of the women disciples, as Peter was the leader of the men. It is also obvious that when the male disciples abandoned Jesus at the end, the women, led by Mary of Magdala, remained faithful. It is also clear that the women seemed closer to the mind of Jesus about his role and message than the men were. Finally, it is clear that Mary and her companions were the first witnesses of the Resurrection, the first proclaimers and preachers of the Christian message, and the ones who went to retrieve the men after the Resurrection, thus laying the foundation stones of Christianity. In other words, it is not difficult to call Mary of Magdala and her companions the true founders of the Christian Church.

How then, are we left with a sinful woman in rags, weeping for her sexual sins, with her true biblical identity obliterated? Why, here in Ireland, are we speaking of Magdalene laundries, rather than of a Church where Mary of Magdala is recognised for what she truly is – founder, apostle and faithful disciple?

As we have seen above, there are traces of the diminishment of the women disciples already in Luke. This process continued as the Church was gradually institutionalised, and the role of the male disciples and apostles became paramount. It was not until the reign of Pope Gregory I at the turn of the seventh century (he died in 604) that the person of the real Mary of Magdala disappeared, and she accumulated to herself the personas of many of the other nameless women of the gospel stories. Pope Gregory, in his pastoral care for the Church, thought that there were too many women figures in the gospels. He reduced them to two, Mary the Mother of Jesus, who was beyond imitation, and Mary the sinner woman, particularly the sinner woman of Luke's chapter seven, with her long hair and tears and on her knees, repenting for her presumably sexual sins. This is Mary, the Magdalene, the sinner woman, who has become a central figure in Christianity, even though she is totally fictional. It was a brilliant move on the pope's part, and is as popular today as it has been down through the ages. It destroyed forever the possibility that Mary of Magdala would be recognised as one of the foundation stones of the church, and established forever the suspicion that every woman was similarly a temptress.

We will be following these two women throughout these chapters as they continue to influence the lives of women in the Churches, as they continue to make sure that women, the majority of Christian believers, are truly the elephant in the Church – there but rarely seen as themselves, but as faint and permanently silenced images of the two Mary's.

Women and Monasticism
in the Fourth Century

Although it may seem like a great historical leap from biblical times to the fourth century, in the case of women's history, this is not necessarily true. In society generally, but especially in the Christian Church, women were considered to be historical accidents and historically negligible. They were seen as part of nature, like the sun or the planets, and one did not write the history of nature at that time unless the normal and expected stream of events was interrupted. Hence, we know about eclipses and floods and other accidental phenomena. And we know of the 'evil' women who did not follow the prescribed roles. The Christian life of women was regarded as a kind of natural phenomenon. They existed in private, below the radar, so to speak; they did not make choices about their own lives and did not come to public attention, unless something extraordinary had occurred. Since the Christian Church had become a male bastion by the end of the first century, women's lives were subsumed under those of men. It is not illogical, then, in such patriarchal arrangements, to see the history of women, when women came to public attention, as an intrusion into male affairs.

Men were the historians and thus imposed various principles of continuity and interpretation on their affairs. Whether it was the invocation of the action of the Holy Spirit, or the imposed principle of apostolic succession, men were intent on illustrating the principle of logical continuity in the leadership and governance of the Church, and in the continuing interpretation of its theological life. God's actions were neither frivolous nor inconsistent.

Women had no such apparent principle. They were not in charge of the interpretation of the affairs of God, theoretically. In fact, they had little means of tracing their history, even if they wanted to. The history of women then, seems spasmodic, discontinuous and almost irrational. There seems little connection between the various 'intrusions' of women into the ecclesiastical world of men. Women too, did not know their history – how could they, without access to education, libraries, and annalists. The fourth century women knew little of their biblical women ancestors, with the exception of the few names that had become stereotypically part of the story, such as the Blessed Virgin and Mary Magdalene, as well as Martha and Mary of Bethany, who was consistently confused with Mary Magdalene. The names had become more symbols of expected womanly virtues than representatives of real historical figures.

And so the leap to the fourth century is a leap to the next fairly coordinated chapter in the history of women in the Christian Church, as this history has been allowed to percolate through the mists of history. But women had not disappeared from the scene. The Apocrypha and Gnostic writings, as well as the tirades of Irenaeus and Tertullian against women illustrate their presence very well. There was obviously an ongoing and vigorous attempt by women to maintain some kind of public role within Christianity, but it is also clear that any attempt to assume leadership roles, to teach or preach or prophesy, was deemed by the 'orthodox' male leaders as heretical. In this way, from almost the very beginning of the institutionalisation of Christianity, women were deemed to be more prone to heresy than men.

By the time of Irenaeus and Tertullian in the second century, Christianity was becoming conscious of how it appeared to the rest of the Roman Empire. And it was the behaviour of women who refused to accept their lot as confined to the household that most seemed to damage the reputation of the Christian Church. The strictures in Paul and Deutero-Paul were repeated constantly, and the fact that women might be responding to the call of God was totally discounted. What God wanted from women, primarily, was submission and obedience. Women who, whatever their role in life, were not ready to accept this lot, were obviously flying in the face of God's will for them.

There were two areas, however, where women were seen to shine in the Christian Church and totally confound male Christian and pagan expectations of the nature of women's activity. These were martyrdom and a life of virginity – that is total sexual renunciation. These were total novelties in the lives of women, and it was not long before the male Christian leaders began to exploit the publicity value of women who chose either lot. The practice of perpetual virginity will occupy us for the rest of this chapter, but it is appropriate to spend a few moments looking at the horrific phenomenon of Christian martyrdom, as it affected women. Since the developing interpretation of the death of Jesus as reparatory, the notion of suffering as a meritorious act had been central to Christianity. The First Letter to Timothy and the Letter of Peter, both by unknown authors, had pointed out, especially to slaves and wives, the usual recipients of household violence, that suffering unjustly was vastly more meritorious than suffering justly or accidental suffering. As we have seen, Christian pastors and theologians rarely saw fit to challenge the right of masters and husbands to enact such violence. Augustine of Hippo writes almost sentimentally about the bruises his mother Monica shared with her friends, bruises inflicted by their husbands. But the public violence of the Empire against the Church was another matter, and when the sporadic persecutions broke out in various parts of the Christian world, from the attacks of Nero in the mid-first century to the final and most widespread persecution of Diocletian in the early-fourth century, the spectacle of the public torture and death of Christians, both women and men, slave and free-born, became almost commonplace throughout the Roman Empire. And it was particularly the courage of women, unexpected and almost unnatural, that became the glory of the Christian community. More particularly, the virgin martyrs brought to the attention of the Empire an extraordinary, new phenomenon – young women who had conquered the 'weakness' of their sex in two ways, by total sexual renunciation and by persisting in their faith despite the most horrific torture and death.

The story of Perpetua and her slave, Felicity, and their martyrdom with several others in the gladiatorial arena in Carthage is typical of these stories. What is most significant about Perpetua's story is that we have her own account of her life in prison, awaiting death, written by her own hand. This document, *The Passion of Saints Perpetua and Felicity,* is the earliest Christian document we have from the hand of a woman. After her execution *c.*203 CE, it was edited and completed, apparently by Tertullian. The document reveals the unbounded faith of these catechumens in their early twenties as they cheerfully await both baptism and death. Perpetua is fully aware of the theology of martyrdom, giving access immediately to the presence of God. The dignity and courage of these young Christians, both female and male, in the face of the most horrible tortures, is endlessly inspiring and also horrifying. No wonder the Christian leadership presented these women to the pagan world as a new breed of womanhood. What is particularly poignant about Perpetua's story is that she was a young mother breast-feeding her baby son in prison, and that her slave, Felicity, was pregnant and very close to giving birth. Perpetua had turned the Roman and Christian family structure upside down by defying her father in order to join the group of catechumens. The father was brought to the prison to make Perpetua do what was expected of her in every institution of the Roman and Christian communities – namely, obey her father. But Perpetua disowned him and declared that her new name was 'Christian'.

Perpetua and her companions went on to be attacked by animals in the arena, for the pleasure of the populace, and she was finally dispatched by a sword wielding gladiator. We know so little about the early years of Christianity that such accounts as that of Perpetua are extremely valuable in revealing the charismatic theology of martyrdom all through the Empire, but also in showing that the Christian Church had completely adopted the pagan Roman model of family, with its household slaves and submissive, faceless women. It is astonishing that the bold, outspoken and dignified voice of Perpetua has survived. When Perpetua told her father, 'My name is now "Christian". I am no longer your daughter,' she was delegitimising this whole structure. Thousands of women would continue to do this down through the ages, though each age of patriarchal Christian authority put their best efforts into re-domesticating the women.

Christianity became one of the legitimate religions of the Roman Empire during the reign of Emperor Constantine in the early part of the fourth century, and, by century's end, Christianity was the only legitimate religion of the Empire. Actually, one can say Catholic Christianity here, as, throughout the fourth century, it fought a ceaseless war against Arian Christianity. The battle had been fought at the Council of Nicaea in 325, and the great Western Catholic Fathers of the Church, whose names are still familiar to us, and will dominate this chapter of women's Christian history, laid the foundations of the Latin Catholic Church, of its theology, and, above all, of its attitude to women. These men were Athanasius, Ambrose, Jerome and Augustine – most especially the last three.

The beginnings of monasticism are shrouded in mystery, but the name of Antony, the first hermit, and Pachomius, the founder of the first cenobitic or communal form of monasticism, have remained as the flagship founders as they 'withdrew' to find God in the Egyptian desert. This is not the place to recount the history of monasticism, but it is the *Life of Antony,* brought apparently to Rome by Athanasius, the great Nicene hero, that seems first to have awakened in the desertless West longing for such a life. Athanasius was constantly being exiled by Arian Emperors and it is during one such exile to Rome that he gave a copy of the *Life of Antony* to a group of women in Rome, led by the widow, Marcella. From at least the first century, some women had been choosing a life of solitary virginity within the Christian communities. This was an individual choice, lived out, for the most part in the confines of the woman's room, and as is obvious, could only be chosen by women of the wealthy Roman and imperial aristocracy. In Rome itself, it seems fairly clear that many males from aristocratic families remained as catechumens, seeing the full Christian life as too harsh and demanding. The aristocratic women, however, had no such qualms and flocked to Christianity in huge numbers. Many were widows as young as twelve or thirteen, and, as the thirst for urban ascetic Christianity spread, the women began to gather in groups on the Aventine Hill in Rome. It was said that there was a veritable 'epidemic of virginity' in Rome and Milan, as well as throughout the whole Empire. It is these two cities which will mostly occupy our attention, that is the cities of Jerome and Ambrose respectively.

The development of total sexual renunciation within Christianity is an astonishing phenomenon, especially as it became the ecclesiastically preferred lifestyle for women right down to our own time. It raises the question of what kind of human person does total sexual renunciation imply. What did Christianity then and now think of women? One of the responses – that Christianity was responding to the decadent morals of the Roman Empire – cannot be maintained. We now know that sexuality was highly regulated in the Empire, especially among the aristocracy. Women, especially, were closely guarded both before and after marriage, as the purity of the male bloodline became the central priority. Within a well-regulated household, the male master was entirely free to use the bodies of the slaves he owned, and, when Christianity fully adopted slavery, this was one of the double standards it maintained. Women had no such option, and it is clear that within Roman marriages, both Christian and pagan, marital sex was a comparative rarity. Each woman was expected to produce about five living children in order to maintain a stable population. When only about four per cent of the population had a life expectancy of fifty, this was a serious civic duty. In this context, total sexual renunciation and the refusal to marry was seen as an extremely odd, and even unpatriotic, choice. But, for Christianity, as we shall see, it became a wonderful gift of propaganda, distinguishing the Christian community from its pagan surroundings. As the age of martyrdom passed, and as Christianity became a mandated religion for all, total sexual renunciation and the ascetic life that surrounded the choice of virginity, became the 'white martyrdom'. Later, we shall explore what this attitude did to the notion of Christian marriage.

One of the first Christian virgins we hear about in Christian history, that is after the martyr period, is Marcellina, the sister of Ambrose, bishop of Milan. We know her only through her brother's writings, but Ambrose was one of the main supporters of Christian virgins, and one of the main haters of the human body and its sexuality. Ambrose had been forced to become bishop of Milan at a time when Arian and Catholic tensions were at their highest. He restored order to the Catholic community and ever after conceived a hatred of Arianism and all forms of heresy. Heresy and sex became linked in his theology, just as virginity and the pure Catholic tradition also became linked. It was while listening to the preaching of Ambrose that the young Augustine came to the conclusion that there was no place for sex within the Catholic tradition.

These sermons of Ambrose focused, in particular, on the unity and undividedness of the Catholic tradition. And, as the numbers of virginal women grew in the major cities of the Roman Empire, his admiration for these young women knew no bounds. Bishop Ambrose, however, knew that the women needed protection as well as admiration. They needed to be limited in their choices as well as encouraged in their asceticism. And it was Ambrose, more than anyone else, who discovered and promoted the Virgin Mary as the supreme model of virgins. Devotion to Mary had not yet become a central feature of Catholic Christian life. It is the last quarter of the fourth century and precedes the Council of Ephesus in 431, and the outpouring of Marian interest that it aroused. But the teaching of Ambrose prepared the way for all further Marian devotion. He ransacked the scriptures and used every conceivable image to illustrate the role of Mary as model of an undivided Church, and the female undivided and unpenetrated body. She was the 'garden enclosed', the 'tower of ivory' and all the other descriptive epithets that are familiar to an older generation of Catholics in the Litany of Loreto.

But above all, it was Ambrose who expanded the doctrine of Mary's virginity to include her perpetual virginity. In one sense, he could do no less. There were already, at the end of the fourth century, real live perpetual virgins in every city. Jerome tells us that it was Eustochium, who was the first virgin from the cradle, so to speak, as we shall see, as many of the original virgins had been widows.

Ambrose spoke of Mary, the *virgo intacta* as the model of the Catholic Church free of all heresy. The body of Mary had never been penetrated by lust or any kind of sexuality. The body of Jesus was wholly pure, as no sexuality whatsoever had been involved in his conception and birth. Similarly, the Catholic Church was a pure unspotted body, untouched by any form of heresy. In this context, then, it became necessary for some of the biblical data to be reconfigured. Since Mary was now a perpetual virgin, the biblical brothers and sisters of Jesus were reconstituted as children of Joseph from a former marriage, or part of a large extended family of cousins and other relatives. A huge glow of holy purity surrounded Mary and Jesus, and their bodies were as unlike all other human bodies as possible.

What is going on here? What kind of human person is envisaged as sexual renunciation becomes the preferred form of human life? What kind of woman is Ambrose talking about? It is clear from the writing of Ambrose, and Augustine later, as we shall see, that the essence of Christian virtue is control of one's body and one's senses. It is the uncontrollability of sexual desire that deeply troubled these men, the fact that their bodies moved of their own accord, beyond their mental and spiritual control. Even though they deeply admired the virgins, they never quite trusted them to live the lives they professed to live. Paul's distinction between spirit and flesh was now reduced to a wholly sexual connotation, which had not at all been the apostle's intention.

There were to be no 'admixtures', no pollution either of the human body or of the body of the Church. As Augustine had picked up from the sermons of Ambrose, even the normal marriage was shrouded in sin, a thought he developed with such enormous consequences for the future of Christian theology, and even more of Christian life. It was the source of Augustine's famous prayer, 'Make me pure but *noli modo*', not quite yet. For Paul, a unified Church depended on a unified household, under the rule of the father, and with silent and submissive wives and children. For Ambrose, Jerome and Augustine, a unified church was mirrored in the lives of virgins, especially in the intact virginity of the perpetual virgin, Mary, and all her followers.

For Ambrose and his followers, Jesus had no sexual origin. He was totally removed from what they called the 'hot little act' that brought everyone else into the world. Jesus, therefore, had to spend no time battling concupiscence. He was totally free of all sexual desire. Ambrose's assertion of the perpetual virginity of Mary – and of Jesus – was a new teaching, that the world seemed ready for. As the reputation of the virgins grew, there was a huge development of writing about the conduct of their lives, and a huge development in the celebration of public liturgies to mark the various stages of their virginal quest.

The next question was 'what about the men, especially the clergy?' Here there was always high theory but little actual practice. Most clergy were married and this continued until the time of Pope Gregory VII in the eleventh century, when marriage became a legal impossibility for clergy. Though marriage was now legally impossible, this opened the door to clerical concubinage, which was common at every level of the church. Pope Siricius, a contemporary of Ambrose, tried in 384 to impose a practice of no intercourse on the clergy, or at the very least, none on the eve of celebrating the Sunday Eucharist, and this was repeated, with little effect, down through the centuries.

Ambrose's women virgins get names and faces in the writings of Jerome, and the implications of Ambrose's teachings are expanded by Augustine, as he mines the story of Adam and Eve, and makes the

37

connection between sexual intercourse and original sin. But first to Jerome. As we have indicated so often, women do not have a history, either in the religious or secular worlds. They are left to lurk somewhere at the edges of men's history. But every so often, they 'intrude' and for a generation or two, become the central focus of the Church's attention. Male Church leaders rush to the barricades, and the result usually spells out even more misfortune for women, theologically and practically. In the fourth century, as we have seen, Ambrose of Milan was so exhilarated by their intrusion as virgins that he was driven to inaugurate a whole new ecclesiology based on his newly-articulated perpetual virginity of Mary. This new doctrine had enormous and negative consequences for women throughout succeeding centuries, and introduced a whole new wave of disgust and abhorrence of the human body. Augustine of Hippo further expanded this theology into his abhorrence of women and his teaching on original sin. But it is primarily in the pages of Jerome, his letters and tracts, in particular, that we actually meet these women face to face, and learn their names and something of their lives. We rarely hear their voices, however, as the voice of a woman was not seen as constituting a part of the historical record or the Church's current life. As has happened throughout Christian history, the women had long since begun to organise their own lives, before the 'Church Fathers' became aware of them.

A good fifty years before the baptism of Augustine by Ambrose of Milan in 386, some women in Rome had begun organising their lives in response to the Gospel command, 'Go sell what you have ...' Sometime in the 330s, Athanasius, the 'hammer of heretics', had arrived in Rome as part of his exile – one of many such – after the Council of Nicaea. He stayed at the house of Marcella on the Aventine and told Marcella and her friends about the peopling of the Egyptian and Syrian deserts with hermits, both women and men, who were trying to live the Gospel fully. He had brought with him the *Life of Antony,* reputedly the first hermit, and this text became the lifeblood of the burgeoning Roman community of ascetic women. As far as we can know, these were the first 'nuns' in the western Church. Marcella was a young widow, still in her teens. Her family had arranged another beneficial marriage for her, but she is reported to have told them, 'If I wanted to marry again, I would marry a man, not an inheritance.' We know so little of the lives of such women that each small indication of their character may be overrated, but this reply gives us some sense of a young woman ready to challenge a whole cultural expectation that she would remarry and bear children. Marcella was joined in her house/convent by Paula the Elder, also a widow and her children Paula the Younger, Blesilla and Eustochium, as well as several others whose names have not been recorded. These women began to live a quasi-monastic life in their own homes. They lived simply, seem to have disbursed at least some of their wealth, prayed the psalms together, studied theology, and entertained whatever wandering or exiled teachers and preachers who passed through Rome. They organised their own life and seem to have recognised the leadership of Marcella.

These women had been living the ascetic life in Rome for about forty years before Jerome arrived in the city in 382, fresh from two relatively uneasy years in the Syrian desert of Chalcis. Jerome arrived in Rome like a thunderbolt. With the decline of persecution, it seemed to him and to several popes, especially Pope Siricius, that the city was full of 'baptised pagans'. As we saw, many men postponed baptism until their deathbed, and many of the clergy, according to Jerome and others, simply haunted the houses of widows looking for an inheritance. Jerome criticised these clergy savagely – as he was wont to do – describing their mincing steps over mud and puddles so as not to dirty their footwear, for example. But it was Jerome's friendship with the women around Marcella and Paula that both introduces us to the lives of these women and brings about Jerome's own downfall in Rome. In his spare time, Jerome was also acting as secretary to Pope Damasus and involved in his monumental work of translating the whole of the Scriptures into Latin.

Jerome had studied Hebrew, knew both Latin and Greek and was in correspondence with many of the great figures of the age. He unleashed this erudition on the women who had 'become virgins'. He taught them to sing the psalms in the original Hebrew, and tells us that they did so without a trace of an accent. It is easy to understand how the women would have lapped up such teaching, not available to them elsewhere, but Jerome, as we learn from his brilliant letters, had a very unbalanced personality. He seems to have loved these women virgins, but he hated womanhood in general and despised their bodies and their sexuality. As we have seen, this was not unusual, but Jerome's temperament was so intemperate that his writings often veered into ridicule and outright misogyny. Like Origen before him, Jerome and other Greek Church Fathers such as Ephraim and Gregory of Nyssa, believed that the minds and souls of women and men were equal, once the disqualification of sex had been removed. He found such minds among the ascetic women of Rome and lauded them to the skies, saying that they had hearts in which a whole library of books was stored. But he found no resonance among the Roman clergy. It is not surprising, then, that Jerome's sojourn in Rome lasted a mere three years, from 382–385. Eventually he was accused of heresy and mingling excessively with the women. He moved to Bethlehem accompanied by Paula and her daughter, whose wealth was sufficient to build two monasteries. Here, Jerome spent the ten happiest years of his life, while he continued to write and get involved in every religious controversy of the time.

The women continued, but their lives became more and more bounded by regulation and religious rule until they disappear as individuals from the Christian story. All three men exercised huge influence on these women and made it impossible for them to continue as an independent group in the Church. Ambrose's teaching on Mary, and especially on her perpetual virginity made her 'as unlike all other women as possible'. She became the model for all other ascetic women, but also a kind of weapon to beat them into obedience and submission. Jerome's behaviour had raised suspicions about the women and led to an increasing enclosure and regulation of their lives. But it was primarily the writing and teaching of Augustine, as he interpreted the Christian message based on his own fractured experience of sexuality that led to the real diminishment of women's virginal lives for hundreds of years.

For Jerome, the body was like a dark forest with raging beasts ready to spring forth at any moment. He writes about his dreams of the 'dancing girls of Rome' that he had met there in his student days. And always, for all three men, whether in Rome, Milan or Hippo, there was that 'hot little act' which is how they described the moment of conception for every human being, with the exception of Mary and Jesus. It was the spontaneity and uncontrollableness of sex that really disturbed them. For all three, marriage was always to be a suspicious way of life – even a good marriage could not be trusted. The more the sexualised bodies of women and men disgusted them, the more they elevated the unsexualised bodies of Jesus and Mary, and the more their understanding of holiness became dehumanised. 'Let the pagans copulate', said Augustine, 'and we will convert their children to virginity.' All three men raised the level of sexual anxiety in the West, and played their part in corrupting the notion of Incarnation, and removing from the human persons of Jesus and Mary all traces of that most human impulse, the impulse to marry and produce children. It was not only women who were now at risk, but those defined then as homosexuals. In the year 390, the historic first burning of homosexual men from the brothels took place in Rome. This was one of the first horrific signs of the growing Christian neurosis about the human body and its sexual functioning, which continues, though with less horrific results, to this day.

While Jerome was in Rome for three tumultuous years, he mixed freely with the women who had become virgins and were gathered in Marcella's house or elsewhere. He saw the women as his intellectual and spiritual equals, once sex had been removed from the equation. He poured utter scorn on any other clergy who dared to do likewise. His letters are a delightful read as he plunges wholeheartedly into the promotion of asceticism in Rome. But all did not always go well.

41

He tells us that Eustochiun was the first virgin from the cradle, so to speak, and lauded her accordingly. Another protégée of his, Blesilla, a young woman barely out of her teens, did not fare so well. She responded to Jerome's ascetic direction so thoroughly that she was dead within the year. Rome was outraged, but Jerome insisted on seeing the event as something of a victory for virginal asceticism.

After Jerome had left Rome – or was expelled from the city – several controversies erupted about asceticism and he jumped in with total enthusiasm to denounce those who questioned the value of such practices. One 'heresy' was a new articulation of the old Origenist controversies about the human person. Jerome completely betrayed the women he had once supported and, in completely sexualising Paul's old spirit/flesh dualism, he began to preach the eternal and unbridgeable distance between women and men. Jovinian and Helvidius, his contemporaries, in their turn, raised questions about the nature of baptism as the most important Christian event, and the use of the virginity of Mary as a model for all. God's grace is open to all, they insisted. Baptism opens the way for all Christians to approach the Divine, and all women, whether virgin, wife or widow, are equally welcome in God's presence. Today, this seems like fairly middle-of-the-road Christian teaching, but in the fourth century age of asceticism, this was seen as heretical. Even some of Jerome's supporters back in Rome, like Marcella and her friends, were shocked at Jerome's excessive stance and language in his *Ante Jovinianum,* and tried to have the writing suppressed. All this was while Jerome was enjoying the money and ministrations of the two Paulas, mother and daughter, in Bethlehem. Interestingly, one of Jerome's conclusions was that only with resurrected bodies could women and men interact without danger, and all other gospel and epistolary statements about love and community were transferred into that indefinite future time. Among the passages thus seen as referring only to the future heavenly angelic life was Gal 3:26–28, which talked of the erasure of distinctions after baptism.

Both Ambrose and Jerome placed huge symbolic weight on the enclosed and intact bodies of women as symbols of a pure Church free of all taint of heresy. Augustine of Hippo joined the troika of Church Fathers from his Episcopal see in North Africa. The threesome did not like or admire each other. 'Another self satisfied mediocrity has arisen in the West' was Augustine's comment on Jerome. Jerome despised Augustine for his lack of Greek, and Ambrose, even though he had baptised Augustine in 386 in Milan, led him to believe that sexuality and Christianity were mutually exclusive.

Augustine had taught in Rome for some time before going to Milan to hear the sermons of Ambrose. As his conversion to Christianity developed, he sent his faithful concubine home and seems to have only gradually given up sexual activity. It is clear that Augustine and his concubine (nameless and faceless as is normal for women in Christian history) practiced artificial contraception. Their two-decade relationship produced one son, Adeodatus, who later became part of Augustine's monastic community. Augustine's presence in Christianity is so overpowering that one can easily forget that the man was sexually dysfunctional. Once he became Christian, and within a few years Bishop of Hippo, Augustine lived in a totally male world. He tells us himself that he did not allow even his female relatives to enter his Episcopal quarters. As Pope John XXIII tells us about his own life, Augustine lived 'as if there were no women in the world'. This did not stop him from writing about women, however, and his teaching on the subject has remained, almost without alteration, as the official teaching of the Roman Catholic Church on women.

Here I will mention only two main points. First of all, Augustine completely expanded the Creation Story of Adam and Eve, as one of the foundational building blocks of Christianity – far beyond the Jewish understanding of the event. For Augustine, this was the beginning of original sin in the first sinful act of intercourse between Adam and Eve. This original sin was passed on, generation after generation, in the act of intercourse which heralded the birth of every human being. Also for Augustine, the root cause of all this sin was Eve's act of disobedience. For the Bishop of Hippo, all Christian activity was rooted in control of one's 'concupiscence', those sexual desires and urges which constantly rose unbidden in the human being. Controlling such urges was the essence of Christian morality for Augustine, and he thought, towards the end of his life, that he had reached some kind of equilibrium, when he reduced his nocturnal emissions to three annually.

Like his two contemporaries, he raised the level of Christian sexual anxiety for centuries. All sexual enjoyment was seen as sinful and as far as possible, all sexual activity should take place under the stern control of the will.

Secondly, Augustine realised that if the Catholic Church taught that God had created women, then women had to be welcomed as members of the Church, but in a very controlled environment. Augustine was wholeheartedly patriarchal in his approach. Women were to be silent and submissive, but not regarded as inferior to men. They had their own role to play in the Divine plan of Creation. Almost 1,700 years later, Pope John Paul II called this role 'ontological complementarity'. Women, in their very beings, were seen as complementary to men. Women's roles and men's roles were distinctly different, prescribed by generation after generation since the early fifth century. The hubbub about the washing of the feet of two women on Maundy Thursday by Pope Francis goes right back to the Bishop of Hippo. This stereotyping of women – and of men – forms the essence of Roman Catholic teaching about women.

As Bishop of Hippo, Augustine founded a quasi-monastic community, and for the remainder of his life surrounded himself only with male companions. He felt at home in the old patriarchal world of the Roman Empire, even to the extent of advocating the flogging of disobedient slaves, and calling in the Roman army to crush heretics – the Donatists – when all his persuasion failed. The old Roman world worked for him and the old structured patriarchal household worked too. For Ambrose and Jerome, there was always something sinful about marriage – it was always a very poor choice when virginity was an option. For Augustine, marriage and the patriarchal household was the main building block of society. For Ambrose and Jerome, marriage was a result of the Fall, but for Augustine, Adam and Eve were not ascetic angels, but human beings like us. God intended marriage. It was the disobedience of the first couple, especially of Eve, and the birth of concupiscence, that led to the Fall. God's plan then, is that patriarchal marriage, with men always presiding over women, is the core of the Christian world. Augustine had a huge streak of pessimism. When he looked out at the world he saw a *massa damnata,* a world of original sinners. Nevertheless, for all three men, virginity was the holier choice since sex always disrupts the life of the Christian.

From his North African Episcopal See, Augustine produced an enormously rich and profound output of theological writing, so influential that to this day theologians continue to be classified as Augustinian or Thomistic. Part of the output of Augustine included several writings on virginity, and several rules for such women. In many ways, these rules still form the basis of most official understanding of the religious life.

Augustine saw clearly that even though virginity was a vastly superior way of life, patriarchal marriage was the bedrock of society. He loved the notion of silent, obedient and compliant women leading private lives under the lordship of a husband. For Augustine, marriage was not the problem, it was the disturbance of the will brought on by sexual desire. Hence, when Pelagius arrived on the Roman scene in the early fifth century preaching about free will and the abundant grace of God, Augustine exploded into indignant response. From his own sexual experience, he knew that the will was not free. All his life he had been tormented by what he believed was the uncontrollability of his will in the spontaneous movement of his sexual organs. His new exegesis of the Second Creation Story and his introduction of the notion of original sin, affecting every single human being, seemed to discount totally everything Pelagius had to say about free will. The total lack of sexual urgings in the Virgin Birth and the perpetual virginity of Mary, confirmed this for Augustine – and indeed for many of his followers. For Augustine every human action was a response to the foregoing grace of God – nothing good could be originated in the human being. For Augustine, Mary's obedience was an act of will, and he further elaborated on the 'vow of virginity' that Mary must have taken long prior to the angel's visit. 'How can this be since I am a virgin?' (Lk 1:34) Mary asks the angel, and this phrase along with Augustine's exegesis of it has rung down through the centuries. Thus, Augustine taught, there was only obedience in the conception and birth of Jesus, but for the rest of humankind, the Fall created a permanent principle of division in the person. For Augustine, sexual intercourse always contained the seeds of death. In all three churchmen, women especially were divided into four categories, linked occasionally with the Parable of the Sower, and the fate of the good seed sown on various kinds of soil. First and lowest were the prostitutes (and, one might add concubines), always sunk in their bodies and responding only to its desires. Then were wives, at around thirty per cent of grace, barely skimming the surface of a decent Christian life. Then, at sixty per cent were widows, who had escaped the exigencies of marriage, and finally the virgins, who seemed to live an angelic life compared to all other women.

There were several theologians, of course, who disagreed and letters and theological tracts flew around the Catholic Church of the time, but it was Augustine's theology that prevailed.

A desperate sadness seems to have pervaded the life of Augustine, particularly about marriage. And as the Roman Empire fell around his ears to the 'barbarians', in particular the Vandals, as they invaded his Episcopal City, one can only imagine the depth of sorrow that enveloped him. Augustine died in 430, and Western Christianity opened itself, of necessity, to the third great influence after the Greek and Latin, the Germanic.

So where does all this leave women, virginal or otherwise? It is obvious that Jesus chose both women and men as disciples. It is also obvious that there never was a notion of baptism that excluded women. Even though women were the first to explore the post-resurrection ramifications of the life of Jesus, particularly in the person of Mary

Magdalene, the gospel message was not strong enough to permeate the surrounding culture with its liberating message. Very soon – within twenty years, as we have seen, the male-dominated Roman arrangements took precedence, particularly as it affected the lives of women. For Paul, as for Augustine, patriarchal marriage and the silencing and seclusion of women within the household were preached as the norm. Nothing but silence and obedience was expected of women. The one choice that Christianity seemed to open to women was the choice of a life of virginity. There are signs of this within the Christian tradition from the second century – the women were secluded individually within their homes – but there was no sign of a gathering of women for support or prayer. The martyr period served the Church well for its propaganda value, but did nothing to change attitudes towards women, except for the occasional marveling at the courage of 'mere' women.

It was the gathering together of women in Rome and other cities in the fourth century in communities of virgins, leading their own lives of asceticism and prayer, under their own leadership, that really seemed to have scared the Church. An 'epidemic' of virginity occurred. Christian women throughout the Roman Empire made a choice against patriarchal marriage and for a self-directed life of virginity, in community with other women. That this was happening within the great cities, and not far away in the desert, added to the distress of church leaders. When enthusiasts like Jerome began to treat these women as equal in intellect and spirit, warning bells sounded for people like Augustine. It is obvious also that having observed what the women were doing, people, like Pope Siricius, began asking about the men. This period marks the beginning of a two-thousand-year debate about a male priesthood of imposed celibacy that also continues to this day. Initially, married priests – and most were married – were asked to refrain from sexual intercourse before celebrating the Eucharist, but down through the centuries, as we can see from its constant repetition in Synod after Synod, a life of sexual renunciation, or even occasional renunciation was not normative for the clergy of any rank.

The efforts to contain the religious enthusiasm of the women led also, as we have seen, to the comparative downgrading of the sacrament of baptism and the upgrading of a life of virginity. The baptismal vocation to ministry was reduced after the writings of Augustine, to a desperate attempt to escape the hellfire punishment for original sin. When it came to living a good Christian life, marriage was a very poor second choice – in fact, for most people, not a choice at all. The exploration of the theology of Christian marriage was also delayed for centuries, and is barely beginning, now in the twenty-first century, to be articulated, with scarcely a hint of input from those actually married.

However, it was probably the expansion of the doctrine of Mary's perpetual virginity that did the most, imaginatively, to seal the fate of Christian women. The thorough dehumanising of Jesus and Mary, despite the biblical evidence about their lives, has had a toxic effect on the sexual lives of millions of women down through the generations. For one thing, it means that women have no history, and 'good wives' even less. If you are a good, silent, obedient woman, you have totally disappeared from the story. For centuries, we know almost nothing about the lives of women, and still, today, it is men who dominate in the language, theology and history of the Catholic Church. *The Tablet* (13 April 2013), the weekly journal, has male celibate liturgists, yet again, denouncing the practice of washing the feet of women, despite the fact that it is a pope doing the washing. These priests remind us all, forcefully, that there is a law forbidding the washing of women's feet in the liturgical canon. All this, of course, also ignores the fact of church diversity. Forty years ago, both women and men were having their feet washed freely in Canadian parishes, and probably elsewhere.

One cannot help but wonder what the story of Catholic women might be like if the great women like Marcella, Paula, Macrina, Furia, Asella, and all their fourth-century sisters had been allowed to follow their own lives and not become subject to the dictates of men whose dysfunctional sexual lives formed the basis of their theology, their re-reading of the Scriptures and their understanding of God. Even though we rarely hear their voices, and have to presume their queries of Jerome in his answers, these women were actually doing women's theology and spirituality. No one called them to this except their God. No pope, bishop or male theologian came up with the idea of women freely and willingly choosing to live, work, pray and worship together. It was the ingenuity of the women that did this. And it was the fear of the men that stymied such unexpected spiritual ventures for another few hundred years.

In the fourth century, the perpetual virginity of Mary was used as a weapon to beat the women into submission. As the story continues, the fate of women becomes even more problematic for the Church.

The fourth and fifth centuries are known as the Golden Era of Christianity. And indeed, for a male-clericalised church, they were golden years. But we shall see as we continue our journey, that what is considered 'golden' for men, is usually quite the opposite for women. After this brief 'intrusion' into public Church life, the women are cloistered, silenced, depersonalised, and successfully banished from being a public preoccupation of the official Church.

The Medieval Women Mystics

Before he died in 434, Augustine of Hippo knew that the Vandals were at the gates of his Episcopal city and that the imperial structures around which he had built his life and his whole theological output were crumbling into piles of debris. His often brilliant – but mostly pessimistic – theology lives on, however, to this very day, and continues to influence the Roman Catholic Church's view of human living, human sexuality and, above all, the humanity and spiritual life of women. Augustine was able to use his literary abilities to inculcate his message to a world and a Church that was ready to hear it. The much more optimistic interpretations of Christianity in the writings of Jovinian, Helvidius and Pelagius were deemed to be totally heretical, even though much of their teaching is now seen as entirely orthodox.

The even more orthodox and courageously optimistic lives of the Roman women like Marcella and Paula have been written out of the history of the Church, as much of women's history has been erased. Their contribution to women's religious life has been almost totally forgotten, and their contribution attributed to Augustine, for the most part. It is to form a part of ongoing Church history that the contributions of women will be forgotten, vilified or reproduced under the more 'likely' name of a man.

The next few centuries, though not without their occasional high points, are mainly centuries of turmoil, as the Germanic tribes introduce the 'third element' into Christianity after the Greek and the Latin influences, and as Christianity moves northward and westward and eventually is cut off from its roots by the huge and rapid expansion of Islam. As we move towards the Middle Ages and the next and greatest intrusion of women into Church history, there are but two historical moments that need to be mentioned here.

One is the story of Pope John the Englishwoman, or Pope Joan, as she is more familiarly known. Joan seems to have grown up in the English colony that had gathered around the monastery of Fulda since the days of Boniface's missionary endeavours. She was recognised as a brilliant scholar, and, apparently with her parents' knowledge and approval, she dressed as a young man in order to pursue a scholarly career. After studies in Athens and a spell of teaching in Rome, Joan/John was elected as pope in 855. So far, most of the records agree, both those written before and after the Reformation. She is said to have been pope for almost two and a half years, when, in a procession, she was overcome with labour pains and gave birth to a son. Here, the records diverge wildly. Some say that she was killed on the spot along with her son. Others say that she survived and spent the rest of her life in a convent while her son went on to become Bishop of Ostia. The story has been called farcical, impossible, an anti-Catholic construct of the Protestant Reformation, and pure legend. One is left to examine the evidence and make up one's own mind.

In these precise years there is much confusion about who was pope. Records have been altered, and, apparently, statues disfigured, in order to disprove her presence. There is absolutely no official male recounting in succeeding years that would validate the story. And yet much of the early discussion of Pope Joan's life deals with the immorality of her actions, not with the actual fact of her existence as pope. Much later discussion is anti-Protestant, as some of the Reformation writers use the story of Pope Joan to cast ridicule on the Catholic Church. Some feminist writers are convinced of her existence and her papacy. The argument may never be solved now, but one thing is certain: Joan lived at a time when the idea of a woman pope was possible to entertain. Even if she never existed, the persistence of her story is testimony to the fact that in the mid-ninth century, there were

Christians who would have accepted a woman pope. In fact, as the papacy developed over the next several decades, the existence of a woman pope would seem to be the least of the Church's troubles. Popes married, had children, killed off rivals, dug up predecessors to further desecrate their bodies, and Marozia, the prostitute, mistress and mother of popes was involved in the lives of the next eight popes.

So whether or not there ever was a Pope Joan – and I rather believe that there was – her papal ministry, apart from the 'scandalous' fact that she was a woman, seems to have been without blemish in the context of that time.

The other anomaly concerning women from around the tenth century onward was the strange existence of women who have come to be called the 'quasi-episcopal abbesses'. Strange to our generation but not to the tenth century. It is important to emphasise here that we are dealing with women from the wealthy land-owning upper classes of society. The vast majority of women – as of men – have disappeared from history, without a trace as they struggled to survive amid war, famine, ignorance and abuse of all kinds. We know so little of women who buried four of their five children, of women who were raped and murdered as acts of war, of women and their children who simply starved to death in the turbulence of the age.

The religious and monastic life – particularly the Benedictine monastic form – had spread widely all over Europe. Benedictine monasteries for women and men took the form of a large village, with all the necessities of life, including infirmaries, hospitality, and shelter in time of war and famine. The abbess or abbot was like a feudal lord/lady receiving the tithes and taxes of their tenant farmers and in return offering a kind of oversight to their lives. It seems to have been Pope Gregory I, whom we have met before, who extended what was called 'exemption' to all the Benedictine monasteries, male and female. That meant that the monasteries were not subject to the local bishop, and more importantly, could keep whatever they produced and were free of the Episcopal taxes. This remained controversial throughout history and still pertains, to some extent. It is in the context of this 'exemption' that we begin to hear about these quasi-episcopal abbesses all across Europe. The women exercised Episcopal power, used the symbols of this power – ring, crozier, mitre – and had jurisdiction over all the people and clergy in their territories. The abbesses were ordained to this position, but no example of such a ceremony survives. As far as we know, they did not celebrate the Eucharist or ordain clergy, but had the power to lead, otherwise, full Episcopal lives, issuing decrees, raising armies, calling and presiding over church councils, challenging emperors and other rulers, and also appointing clergy and hearing confessions.

Many of these great abbeys remain in actuality and in memory to this day, though the names of their great women rulers are usually forgotten. The ruins of the great abbey of Hilda at Whitby remain, even as the backdrop to Heartbeat, a contemporary television drama. In France, the royal abbey of Jouarre continued until it was suppressed by the French Revolution. In Germany, the abbesses of the Quedlinburg monastery ruled over the whole town, and the abbey was also suppressed by the Reformation. The great abbey of Las Huelgas de Burgos in Spain continued until the beginning of the nineteenth century and spread its influence all over northern Spain.

This is but a brief summary of a monastic structure that gave to women an opportunity to legislate, make and break liturgical regulations and provide shelter and spiritual sustenance to thousands of women, and often their dependent families in times of war and famine. These monasteries ran famous schools, and were the chief institutions of theological education in their territories. The monasteries, as far as canon law was concerned, came under the heading of 'nullius diocesis', that is, they were under the rule of no bishop and did not belong to any diocese.

The turbulence of the ninth and tenth centuries in the Christian Church gave space for much diversity. In every era, when the normal rules of discourse and behaviour break down, the roles of women are expanded. Women always have seemed to take the opportunity to move out from under patriarchal dominance, when the world or the church is in turmoil. Contrariwise, when the centralisation becomes too great and the oppression and restriction of women and others becomes too burdensome, something eventually gives and women and the poor 'intrude' on people's consciousness in a new way. These are but two of the many explanations given for the emergence and vast intrusion of the women mystics in the period of *c*.1150 to *c*.1450. We have come across the names of many great women whose existence and contribution we know about, but from whom we have no word or authentic voice. All this changes with the arrival of the women mystics. Although they were eventually terrorised into silence and much of their writing destroyed, we still have sufficient information to recognise these women as brilliant, poetic, theologically innovative and an utterly radical challenge to the mainstream, or 'malestream', Christian church. But first, some context is necessary.

By the year 1000 most of Europe had been evangelised, often by force. The foundation of the great Abbey of Cluny at the beginning of the tenth century had begun the renewal of monastic life, but it was not until the arrival of Hildebrand as Pope Gregory VII in 1073 that the centralisation and reform of the clergy began in earnest. Up until this time many, if not most, popes, bishops and priests had been married, even though there had been a long tradition advocating celibacy. Hildebrand forbade marriage to all the ordained and strove by every means in his power to break up the (legal) marriages of clergy and dispose of the wives and children, often by being sold into slavery. The great divide between clergy and laity had begun, and, as the emphasis on priestly celibacy rose, the emphasis on the dangers of women also increased. We are back to the days of Augustine, who had not allowed any contact with women, even female relatives, and forward to the days of Pope John XXIII, who said that he lived 'as if there were no women in the world'. All future reforms emphasised the distinctiveness of the priestly role, and as the reforming councils did their work on the sacraments of Eucharist and Penance, the priest took on the guise of a sacred personality.

Part of this reform was the emphasis on the ordination of monks, which caused a huge divide between male and female monastics.

Benedictine and other women who had mixed freely with their brother monks were now segregated, and eventually cloistered and shut off from all worldly contact. The role of the pope became more centralised and popes sought to establish their power over emperors and all other rulers. Christendom had arrived, a theocratic state where endless struggles ensued between popes and emperors as each sought to put their authority on a firm footing. Emperors claimed the divine right of kings, whereas popes claimed to be the Vicars of Christ on earth, rather than the successor of Peter, the basis of their authority until then. A great sacralisation of the clergy was taking place, and women were seen as the enemies of this system. The watchword for women was *aut maritus aut murus*, that is, they were always subject to obedience, either to a husband, or behind the walls of a cloistered convent. The total indifference of all popes to the existence and position of married women continued for centuries.

Part of the reform of the clergy entailed their education, and it is partly in this context that the great universities came together throughout the twelfth century. The rediscovery of the works of Aristotle and the discovery that much of traditional Christianity was subject to internal contradictions provided the theological work of the universities for the next several centuries. Debates over the relationship between faith and reason flourished, and theology became more and more abstruse.

Part of the amazingly rich tapestry of the twelfth and thirteenth centuries was the arrival of new male religious orders. The Cistercians, founded by Bernard of Clairvaux, had flourished since the previous century, but now Franciscans, Dominicans, Norbertines and many others appeared on the scene with their own wholly new approaches to the 'following of Christ'.

Some say that it was the return of the few surviving Crusaders from the Holy Land who brought back their awe and revived faith at having been able to follow in the footsteps of Jesus, that regenerated the *vita evangelica,* or a life lived according to the gospels. At any rate, the *vita evangelica* began to flourish all over Europe, and the preaching of the

Gospel, especially by the Franciscans and Dominicans became one of the distinctive new features of the Middle Ages. This whole development was extremely challenging to Western Christendom, especially the teaching on poverty, as the Church and papacy had just begun to experience the benefits of power and wealth, seeing them as God-given gifts.

Women, at the very core of their female being were excluded from this whole development. Women were seen as entirely a negative quantity, constant seducers of men, more prone to heresy, quite incapable of grasping theology, and certainly forbidden to teach or preach. The whole university educational endeavour was forbidden to women, and for centuries their education languished in the realms of chance and oblivion. Of course there were the few exceptions, such as Heloise, the famed companion of Abelard, but without the benefit of a benign male cleric as a relative, women were totally excluded from the main educational developments of the day.

This is the context, then, of the emergence of the medieval women mystics. On the one hand, it would seem to be the worst possible context for such a vast 'intrusion' but, deprived of male spiritual sustenance, the women took charge of their own lives, as the fourth-century women had done. Unfortunately, because of the vagaries of ecclesiastical history, the medieval women would not have known about Paula and Marcella. There was no such thing as a continuous women's history. Each generation had to show ingenuity and invent their own forms of female theology and spirituality. And their ingenuity and brilliance cannot fail to astonish us.

Who were the medieval women mystics? In a very general way, they can be divided into three groups, and, as I describe these groups, I can bring the history of women within the patriarchal structure up to date. We shall return later to the subject of mysticism, as we examine their writings.

First of all were the 'convent mystics', who initially were Cistercian and Benedictine, and later women religious attached to the new male orders of the Franciscans and Dominicans. These were cloistered women, living regular lives of prayer, work, and study and with a fairly regulated liturgical and spiritual life. There was also the great Clare of Assisi (1193–1253), who was the first woman to write a Rule for her followers, and have it accepted by the pope. Among the earliest mystics was the recently-honoured Hildegard of Bingen (1098–1179), who was made a Doctor of the Church by Pope Emeritus Benedict XVI at the end of 2012. We shall return to the astonishing Hildegarde. In the thirteenth century there was a famous monastery in Helfta in Germany, a kind of women's university run by the brilliant Abbess Gertrude for over forty years. From that community we have the writings of Mechtilde of Hackeborn, Mechtilde of Magdeburg and the younger Gertrude of Helfta. The writings of all these women are now easily available in English translation. The convent mystics had the benefit of a regular liturgical and community life. They had access to libraries and the leisure time to pray, read, work and converse together. If they had an abbess like Hildegarde, they had the benefit of her liturgical innovations, her music, her visions, and her very creative rule, as we shall see.

The second group of mystics introduces us to a medieval innovation, the Beguines. No one is quite sure where this vast gathering of women came from. The official Church always feared their independent lifestyle. We know that there were hundreds of Beguines living in the various cities of northern Europe. They were insistent that they were not nuns, because if they were, they would have had to be enclosed. They supported themselves by the work of their own hands, had no great family dowries like the nuns of Helfta, and insisted on travelling from place to place, teaching and preaching in the vernacular. They used vernacular translations of scripture, so that everyone could participate and understand. They accepted only their own women leaders and their own rules. They could leave the group to marry, as their vows were not seen as permanent and solemn. Beguines lived in groups or alone and shocked the church to its very core by their eloquence and courage. The great Beguine mystics are Mechtilde of Magdeburg, who retired to Helfta after a lifetime of travelling and preaching, Marguerite Porete, who was burned at the stake on 1 June 1310, and Hadjwich of Brabant, about whom we know very little except through her writings.

The third group contains all the other individual women who chose the mystical life for a variety of reasons and lived alone or were surrounded by groups of followers. This group includes Catherine of Siena (1347–1380), Julian of Norwich (1342–1416) and Joan of Arc (1412–1431), another astonishing woman burned at the stake at the age of nineteen on 31 May 1431.

Just as the whole theological structure of transubstantiation and forgiveness of sins was established, as well as the essential need for clerical mediation of God's grace for all the non-ordained, the women mystics, individually and as a group, claimed direct immediate access to God, and claimed further that this direct access was available to all without exception. Just as the whole Thomistic structure of faith and reason became the centre of the theological enterprise, the mystics claimed that love was central, and far beyond reason in God's eyes. And just as the Latin language became the sacred language of the increasingly clericalised Church, the women mystics taught, prayed, read the Scriptures, and preached in the new vernacular languages of Europe. As the official male Church became more exclusive and centralised, the women mystics opened up 'Holy Church the Greater', as Marguerite Porete called it, as a loving haven for all. And just as the maleness of the Church as an exclusive patriarchal hierarchy became more and more pronounced, the mystics taught women to pray to God directly, as Mother as well as Father. Their ease with a gendered language about God and gendered prayer to God, struck the medieval male church like a thunderbolt of horror. It is easy to see how these women were seen as such a threat to the newly-centralised and newly-clericalised Church. They did not have a male superior, seemed not to obey anyone, travelled and preached freely, took no solemn vows and generally led their own independent lives totally apart from any cloister. What astonished the Church, however, was the obvious holiness of these women, both in and out of the convent, and for this reason, they were able to survive for about one hundred years without major interference. However, with the execution of Marguerite Porete, the first woman mystic to be executed for heresy, the crackdown intensified and the women were either forced into cloistered convents, executed, or terrorised into silence.

In the early Church, the women were silenced as part of the acknowledged patriarchal custom, in total opposition to the teaching of Jesus. In the fourth century the women were vilified if non-virginal, and cloistered as monastic rules were refined. And now, in the Middle Ages, the women are either executed or terrorised into silence. There is no space for women to be active in the Church on their own initiative, and without male clerical sponsorship and leadership.

We must now look at the subject of women's mysticism, take an all-too-brief look at the contribution of Hildegarde of Bingen, and then, in the next chapter, look at the teaching of Mechtilde of Magdeburg, Catherine of Siena, Julian of Norwich and, finally, Marguerite Porete.

In a church built on clerical mediation, mysticism – which seems to dispense entirely with the mediating clerical ministry – is usually greeted with some suspicion. It was forbidden entirely in the seventeenth century, as part of a huge debate about contemplative prayer and good works between Bishops Bossuet and Fenelon in France. All the more so was the mysticism of women greeted with hostility, especially if they seemed to be obeying the rule of all mystics: 'I obey God not man.'

Mysticism is the experience of direct access to God, and raises all the questions about to whom and when God reveals him/her self. Much of the writing on mysticism takes male mysticism as a norm and then tries to fit the experience of women into that paradigm, usually unsuccessfully. The traditional account of the spiritual journey, based on male experience, started with *purgation* or the cleansing from sin, the supposition being that all dwelt in sin as a matter of course. The next step was *illumination* or the enlightening of the mind and the rendering of all spiritual matters more easily accessible. Finally there was *contemplation,* or the unitive stage when the believer felt totally united with the source of all being, that is called God. Volumes have been written about these stages, always considered normative for all men and women. The words and actions of the women mystics, however, as revealed in their lives and writings, trace a rather different path.

For men, whose lives were built around the choice of a career in the public realm, either in the army, in commerce and the accumulation of wealth, or in the Church, this choice usually entailed a huge conversion experience, a shattering of the ego, a reframing of life's pattern and a total separation from the world, where the temptations to wealth, power and sex abounded. The life of Saint Francis of Assisi offers a perfect example of this male journey. For men, the journey started with the recognition that there was a great gap between them and God, whether intellectually, with a deep experience of original sin, or spiritually, with the realisation that their choices were not conducive to God's presence in their lives. Much of the spiritual journey, presented in monasteries, convents, retreats and spiritual guidance is rooted in this threefold journey, starting out from a sense of sinfulness, even today.

The spiritual journey as delineated by women, speaks of no experience of a gap between God and the human, but a sense that from time eternal God was present and already loving and active in a person's life. There was no sense of original sin, but a sense of what Matthew Fox called 'original grace'. 'Just to be born is grace enough', as so many women mystics have said. The sense one gets from reading the women mystics is that at around the age of five, God became known to them in an experience of love and union. This sense of loving-kindness accompanied them throughout their lives and was responsible for their personal choice to follow God alone. For nearly all women, this ran in opposition to their parents' desire for a suitable marriage and wherever we know the details of their life story, an ensuing battle between parents and child about obedience in a patriarchal household and an independent choice to follow God's call.

The life of Catherine of Siena and so many others illustrates this perfectly. Finally, after years of drawing closer to this God, the women felt that they had to go public, so to speak, and tell the world of this love that had engulfed their lives.

These spiritual journeys of men and women paint an entirely different picture of human beings, of God and of Christian spirituality and theology. The women's journey can be seen as heretical when looked at from the perspective of traditional Christian theology. When looked at, however, from a biblical perspective, it seems to ring true with an evangelical fervour. As the Middle Ages grappled with the newly-preached *evangelica vita,* the women's journey makes abundant sense. This spiritual journey has always existed as a minor chord in Christianity. It had seemed so much easier to see God as Lord and Judge, almost permanently angry and ready to strike down the sinner, than to see God as a loving Mother and Father who has cherished each individual from all eternity.

Mysticism, then, is a form of the spiritual life that, starting from this primal experience of love and union, always seeks more: more insight, more contact, more knowledge, but above all, more love and greater union. One might say that in mysticism, love and knowledge are identical. It is rooted in experience, in the whole bodily sense of contact with God. For women, this entailed taking the *imago dei* seriously, and meant bringing the whole of one's femaleness to the relationship. One might say that for women, mysticism is a form of praying with the integrity of one's whole being. It included a kind of spiritual rejection of the traditional definition of prayer as 'raising the heart and mind to God', that is, away from the sinfulness of one's created being and of the world. For these women, mystical prayer was akin to what ecologists today might call 'breathing with the planet'. There was a sense of the unity of all things, without the graded divisions entailed by a patriarchal and clerical hierarchy. Whereas, the contemplative heights of traditional male mysticism was seen as open only to the very few, the women mystics saw and taught that mysticism was a gift available to all, without exception. These women mystics then, introduce us to a form of Christianity without Eve, original sin, and the whole theological structure of Redemption built on this. For them, Jesus was not needed as a suffering Saviour, but as someone who taught them how to live as full human beings. They had no sense of the traditional dualistic division of body and spirit, but saw the spirit-body unity as precisely the locus of God's presence with them. As so many of the mystics expressed it, 'My real me is God.'

For male mystics, with their abundance of choices in this world, the goal of all mysticism was a union of wills with God. That meant that they had to discover God's will for them and then bend their own will to carrying it out. It was almost like doing spiritual violence to one's self. For women, the goal of all mysticism was the 'public exercise of compassion', that is living the compassion of Jesus fully and publicly. To live in such a way entailed a total challenge to the traditional and universally accepted model of female living in private, *aut maritus aut murus*. One can see how the Church was challenged to its roots. 'Who are these women?' was the totally bewildered question of more than one male theologian. All the questions about women's existence and role were raised again in a context that was just beginning to take shape as a completely male-centralised ecclesiastical structure.

Hildegarde of Bingen

In many ways, the life of the astonishing Hildegarde of Bingen can be seen as a bridge from the hidden lives of most women in the early middle ages to the full flowering of mysticism in the thirteenth and fourteenth century. Hildegarde, born in 1098, was the tenth child in her family, and as such, was given as a tithe to the Church in the person of the woman hermit, Jutta of Sponheim, who was attached to the Benedictine monastery of St Disibode. Hildegarde was around five years of age at the time. With Jutta she absorbed the basics of the spiritual life, including the ability to read Latin, and as their fame grew, followers from all parts of Europe were attracted to them. The hermitage grew into a fully fledged monastery and in her teens

Hildegarde and many other women received the veil from the local Bishop of Bamberg. When Jutta died, the nuns, now following the Benedictine rule, elected Hildegarde as their abbess in 1136. Over the next several years the activities of Hildegarde included not only the care of her monastery, but the writing of several books of theology, several missionary preaching journeys, the writing of hundreds of letters, the illustration and explanation of a whole series of visions, and the cataloguing of the herbs and medications used in the monastic infirmary. The latter task marks Hildegarde as one of the first founders of the science of pharmacy in Europe.

Hildegarde's theology, especially in her first book *Scivias,* is wide-ranging and astonishing. This is not the place for a study of her theology, but she was the first person that we know about who studied in detail the subject of Christian anthropology – that is, what it means to live as male and female human beings. She dealt with this both from a scientific point of view, in her quite unusual study of human sexuality, and from a cosmic spiritual perspective. Hildegarde did not take on her prophetic task lightly, having to break through centuries of condemnation of women's theological writing and teaching. As with so many of the women mystics, Hildegarde tells us that from a very early age, long before she was given to Jutta, she had an awareness of God and knew that she was living in the 'shadow of the Living Light'. This vision stayed with her all her life. Despite her brilliance on many fronts, Hildegarde, in a letter to Bernard of Clairvaux in 1147, describes herself as 'wretched and more than wretched in the name of woman'. This was partly a kind of rhetorical device used by women down through the ages in order to deflect male criticism, but it was also part of her understanding of what being a woman entailed. This was a peculiar mix of Augustine's notion of complementarity, or the diverse roles of women and men ordained by God, and a kind of strange disdain that she professed for the weakness of womanhood. In many ways, her theology of women is entirely contradicted by her life. As we said, she was the very first Christian thinker to tackle the question of what it meant to live as a woman. She looked at the great paradigms of 'femininity', namely Eve, Mary and Mater Ecclesia, or Mother Church. To the extent that she could, Hildegarde was holistic in a very dualistic world.

What did Hildegarde think of God? Her most common names for this great Living Light in which she lived was *Sapientia,* or Lady Wisdom and *Caritas,* Lady Love. The writing of Hildegarde is so symbolic that one can only interpret it as best one can, but Lady Wisdom was, for her, a real personification of the Divine in female form. *Sapientia,* from the Greek *Sophia,* signified the total mystery of Creation and the bond between the Creator and Creation. Like all women mystics, Hildegarde believed in the ultimate redemption of the whole of Creation. *Sapienti* raised especially the question of woman and God, and Hildegarde saw the cosmic image of woman at the heart of the whole divine mystery.

As her celebrity grew, the monastery was inundated with applicants and Hildegarde was forced to move and found a new monastery at Rupersberg, opposite Bingen, the site having been revealed to her in a vision. Once this foundation was in order, Hildegade set out in 1158 on the first of four long preaching journeys, and when she was finished in her late seventies, she had preached in most of the major cities and cathedrals of Germany without any apparent interference. In her eightieth year, Hildegarde suffered one of the greatest trials of her life when she and her community were excommunicated, which meant that no liturgical services could be held in the monastery. The apparent reason was that she gave shelter to, and eventually buried, an excommunicated nobleman, whom she believed to be innocent. Her strong letter of protest to the Bishop of Mainz on this occasion, is a wonderful testimony to her personality and her love for her sisters. After an appeal to the pope, the interdict was lifted. Hildegarde died in 1179 at the age of eighty-two. She was venerated as a saint almost immediately, but, despite many attempts, she was never canonised. Since the 1940s, she has been acknowledged as a saint in all the dioceses of Germany. Shortly before he resigned, Pope Benedict XVI declared her a Doctor of the Church, to join the other three women Doctors, namely Catherine of Siena, Teresa of Avila and Thérèse of Lisieux.

The life of Hildegarde, while astonishing in its intellectual and scientific output, also sets down several markers for the further development of women's mystical life. Hildegarde herself did not write on either the theory of mysticism or on mystical prayer, but her writings are brimful of the female God-images that return again and again in later writings.

Besides her scientific and cosmic writings, Hildegarde was also a very practical Mother Abbess of a monastic community. She wrote liturgies and spiritual dramas for her sisters, encouraged the playing of musical instruments, and designed new habits for her women's community, complaining that the usual men's monastic outfit was not suitable for women who menstruated. In many ways, Hildegarde was so gifted that she rises above her historical context, and cannot be judged on any of the existing male standards of accomplishment. In one of her last visions, she speaks of the 'endless circulation of the energy of love' in the universe and this one phrase unites her explicitly with the great women mystics of the thirteenth and fourteenth centuries, whose central theme was love. Hildegarde often spoke of herself as a 'feather on the breath of God' and this sense of being wafted aloft and soaring is another major theme of later mystics. Hildegarde is one of the very first Christian women to be able to speak to and retain an audience through her writings, and many later women treat her as an authority for their work.

The following pieces sum up some of the writings of Hildegarde. They contain direct words, phrases and sentences from her hand, and point to the central concerns of this great abbess' life.

Womanspirit of God

O Holy Womanspirit,
From you the clouds have their flowing,
The air its movement,
The stones their moisture,
The water spurting forth in streams
And the earth its glorious green verdure.

My God reveals herself in all her beauty
In the mirror of creation,
She flames above the fields to signify the beauty of the earth,
The beautiful earthen matter from which we are all made.
She flames on the waters of the world,
Suffusing the whole water-fed world,
As life suffuses the body.
She burns in the sun and the moon
To show forth our brightness of intellect
And strength of spirit.
She gleams in the stars to show us
The words we may use for praise.

And I,
A feather on the breath of God,
Pray that the Spirit of God
May cleanse me from the malice
That drags me down to earth,
And win me the friendship of God.

When I Was Five

Now I begin to know why I have been struggling,
Now it is becoming clear to me why I have always been a little ill,
Never my true lively energetic self,
Always battling uphill, gasping for breath,
Throat constricted and lungs flailing.

I am beginning to remember when I was five.

Then it was that I was first conscious of a power of holy insight
running through my being.
At five, I was clear-eyed, open-eared, full-voiced.
When I was five they thought it was a childish game.

Now I know that it was you, O God, nourishing my child's spirit.
Ever since childhood,
In the marrow of my bones and the veins of my flesh,
I feel withered.
I am aching to speak,
But a woman's voice is, they say, the voice of demons.
What do we need to hear from a woman, but evil?

And then, finally, my friends, wearied of my excuses.
Volmar and Richardis said enough!
Speak!

I have found a way of speaking
Not in trance, not in heavenly vision, not in mysterious sounds,
I speak through the power of story.
I write pictures, I make visible in paint
that which I see in my prayer.

Now they call me mystic, visionary, holy Abbess,
But it is I, the same Hildegarde.
Nothing in me has changed
Except that I have found my voice.

All I ever wanted was to speak God.
They speak of a singing Trinity;
I see Trinities everywhere.
They speak of a changeless God
I see God in light and discord.
They speak of a distant God,
Far removed from the world of Bingen.
I see God here in my garden,
Outside my window, rising in the juicy sap of the Spring plants.

They speak of a God who thunders,
But I have met a God
Who soars and floats and ripples in the moist air.
And again I know
I am a feather on the breath of God.

Praying at Seventy

All my life, it now seems to me,
I have had clear sight of God.
Like currents of air, spirits gliding upward,
I have been in flight.

The clouds form and reform,
They race across the sky and swell in stillness, all aglowing,
And they say: Remember God!

As my physical eyes fail,
My inner eyes open in wonder.
As my bodily ears strain,
My God-antennae are instantly alert
And announce: She, your God, is here.

As my brain is sometimes befuddled,
My heart leaps in elation at the robin's antics.
As my feet stumble, my spirit races ahead:
Come on, come on, there is so much more.

As my hands grow numb and sometimes sore,
My touch grows softer, sensitive, more grace-filled.
My senses may dim,
But my whole being seems alive,
And shouts: Live it up.

I seem now to be bathed in light.
I say to myself:
'Now I am living in the shadow of the Living Light.'

I used to worry about sin;
Now I have no time for this.

When I pick up the Scriptures,
The light streams out at me.
The words tremble with life,
And shout: 'Abundant Life.'

My memory is memorising:
All the strands are being drawn together.
I can now say:
'I see, I hear, I know, I smile, I love.'

I see new words, hear new music, know in deeper tones,
I smile at my dreams, I love with the trees.

I see bright flames coming from human lips.
I see rippling water flowing in endless light.
No container on earth can keep this flowing.

All my life is now here in the palm of my hand.
I am child, maid, woman, crone.
I live it all, now more fully.
How can I now describe my lightsome life?
I see.
I yearn yet.

The Beguines

Mechtilde of Magdeburg
The life of Mechtilde of Magdeburg is known to us only from the
brief autobiographical comments in her book, *The Flowing Light of
the Godhead*. As the title implies, Mechtilde's God was a flowing God
of light and love. Like most women of history, she remains in a cloud
of anonymity. Despite her brilliant and lyrical writing, it is hard to
grasp who she really was and what kind of personality she had. Her
writing indicates that she stood out significantly from the main
scholastic theologians of her age, despite the fact that she seems to
have been well educated and familiar with both secular and theological
literature.

Mechtilde lived throughout the span of the thirteenth century from
*c.*1208 to *c.*1282. Like most of the medieval women mystics, she tells
us that she knew God intimately from a very early age. She speaks of
'divine greeting' from about the age of twelve. In her early twenties,
she was in Magdeburg as a Beguine, with apparently some
authoritative position in a Beguine community. Mechtilde was very
critical of the clergy and the official institutional church, and spoke
often of God having to turn to the weak and insignificant because the
strong and powerful had let Him down with their corrupt and
immoral lives. Mechtilde travelled frequently, preaching and teaching
and writing in her own German dialect, so that her words would be
available to all. Her book was written over a number of years and the
final section was finished at the women's Cistercian monastery of

Helfta, where she had retired. By then, she was weary, ill and going blind, but appreciated and nurtured by the great mystics of Helfta, Abbess Gertrude, her sister, Mechtilde of Hackeborn and their younger companion, Gertrude the Great. Helfta was a kind of women's university of mysticism and was a perfect environment for Mechtilde in her closing years.

Mechtilde saw her writings as a new vernacular bible for all Christians. She was convinced that her work was directly inspired by God. This was partly a strong personal conviction of Mechtilde's, but also a barrier against the misogynist attitudes of the age, which taught that women could not teach and that the words of women were, in general, more demonic than divine. Four great mystics of the thirteenth century have been named by Bernard McGinn as the four women evangelists – Mechtilde, Hadewijch of Antwerp, Marguerite Porete, and Angela of Foligno. The confidence of these women was amazing. They were convinced that God inspired their work and that it was intended as a new vernacular bible for the whole church at a time when the traditional scriptures were mostly not available to the people. Their writing represented the 'truth of God', and as Mechtilde wrote, 'no one can burn the truth'. This illustrates also that she was fully aware that she, as a woman teacher could be burned to death, but that her words, the words of God, could not be destroyed.

For Mechtilde the very essence of God was 'flowing', a reciprocal process which set up a constant and dynamic relationship between God and the people. What is more, she saw God's *being* and *love* as flowing downhill, past all the powerful and learned men at the top of the hill, to the women and the poor at the bottom. Mechtilde was scornful of many of the 'learned men of Scripture' and wrote that God often saw them as 'fools and charlatans'. One can see that this did not endear her to the clergy, but her Dominican adviser was faithful to her and edited her books for posterity. Because God's *love* and *wisdom* flowed downhill, it was necessarily revealed to a woman and not to a man. The essential place of women in the Church as the recipients of God's renewed message is common to all the mystics. They show little sense of being diminished by their sexual nature or by being daughters of Eve. Indeed, in many ways, their understanding of the Church was of a Christianity without Eve, without a Fall, and certainly with no distancing of a pure and holy God from a sinful people. As with all the mystics, there is a sense that from the very beginning, even before time, women were intimately connected with God. Here we see again that, for these women, there existed an intimacy and an identity with God that is rarely found in the writings of men. The precise and accurate logic of the scholastics is left behind in the glorious, emotive and often erotic language of Mechtilde and her followers. Where the male theologians described the great desertion of God by the human race, as described in the early chapters of Genesis, the women saw no gaps in this relationship which existed from the beginning and revealed itself progressively through life. Where the scholastics argued about faith and reason, the mystics opted for love and intimacy, and saw God as a faithful and ever-present lover.

Even though Mechtilde was familiar with the Scriptures, she spoke too of the Book of Experience and the Books of Love and Compassion, as the sources of her teaching. It was the human presence of Jesus, especially in the Eucharist that gave her and other women a sense of their own humanity and its dignity. Through the Eucharist, they became participants in the humanity of Jesus and it was the imitation of this humanity rather than any sense of Redemption from sinfulness that was the cornerstone of their spirituality and mysticism.

This 'new gospel' was given to 'weak women' by God so that they could teach the learned. It seemed to come naturally to them to claim God as the author of their writing in a way that no male author would, could or had done. In this way, Mechtilde turns the usual theological, spiritual and mystical language upside down. This is truly a new women's theology, which is in continuity with the snatches and remnants of women's lives that remain to us from history. While men struggle with God's will and, in general, God's displeasure with the human race, the women explore the dimensions of God's love. The women do not struggle with conforming themselves to God's will, as the male spiritual directors and theologians indicate, but explore the unfolding of God's perpetual presence in their lives until it blossoms into something like an identity of being.

They explore the 'flowing forth' of all things from God and the return of our lives and witness to the same God. It is an unending ebb and flow, reminiscent of the words of Emily Dickinson, 'The Spirit lurks within the Flesh / Like Tides within the Sea.' This is an unseen and unceasing flowing back and forth between God and humanity that marks our lives irrevocably.

Because of the reality and growing intensity of this love, Mechtilde and later mystics also experience a kind of estrangement from God, where, even with the best will in the world, they are unable to comprehend or experience what is the reality of God's love, its depth and permanence and inviolability. This is a source of great suffering for them, and is often referred to as the great 'abyss' of God's love. In the writings of male theologian and mystics, the metaphor of the 'abyss' is often seen as the source of evil and distance from God. For the women, it is like a womb, giving birth to God in the brilliant darkness and stillness of eternity. This also seems to unite the mystics in a new way to Jesus who 'emptied himself' and leads them to a new experience of union through him.

For all the women mystics, Mechtilde included, their responsibility for the Church, to let the people know the truth of God, was central to their lives. Their mysticism was not for themselves, but for everyone. All could be mystics, God was available to all, but also the poor and neglected, especially the women need to know how close and how available God was to them. Compassion was at the centre of their lives and the 'public expression of compassion' was at the centre of their care for the Church. It has often been suggested that, since women cannot teach or hold authority in the Church, the exercise of private compassion – since women were unconditionally confined to the private and not the public space of Church life – was particularly appropriate to them. This was particularly addressed to mothers and compassion was not always seen as an appropriate virtue for men.

Their role was leadership and decision-making and theological speculation and teaching. The women mystics accepted that compassion was central to a Christian life, but taught that it should be public, the hallmark of every Christian life, from 'pope to peasant' as Augustine of Hippo was wont to say.

The poetry of Mechtilde gives us a real sense of where her spirit lay and where she saw the Spirit of God guiding her. In the following pieces, we get an idea of her teaching, her lyrical skills and her loving theology. Again, many words and phrases come directly from the hand of Mechtilde. One of her favourite reflections was about the birds of the air and the fish in the sea, at home in their own habitat. For us, God is our natural habitat and we can never be removed from this loving and deeply-compassionate space.

Why not soar?

You have the wings of longing,
You know the pull of hope,
You feel the flowing of desire:

So why not soar?

Fish cannot drown in water,
Birds cannot sink in air,
You cannot fall from my sight:

So why not soar?

Woman, I have adorned you,
Woman, I have delighted in you,
Woman, I have made my home within you:

So why not soar?

Be as the dove, I soar in her,
Lighten your heart, I soar in you,
Uplift your being, be an Easter song:

Why not soar?

The Singing Trinity

Have you heard the singing of the Trinity?
The full-throated robust music
That fills the universal air
With rhythmic trembling,
And ripples along spring-flowering branches
With the delicacy of cherry-blossom.

One voice sings:
I am white water,
A restless surging stream
Sparkling, casting light everywhere at once,
Gurgling with the pleasure
Of life and movement
And plunging forward into mystery.

The second voice sings:
I am the running tide,
Flowing and ebbing,
Always in motion, never at rest,
Coming and going
Divine and human, human and divine,
A tide that runs eternally,
With the song of unending love.

The third voice sings:
I am the pulsing of energy
Rising as sap
Bursting as leaf and flower
Reddening as autumn glow,
Fading as seasons change, but always living, feeding, sheltering,
And always showering with the truth of beauty,
The beauty of truth,
The hidden depths of earth.

And so in chorus
The triune voices mingle their songs
In one great chorus.
Listen
And you will hear
The singing of the Trinity.

Lie Down in the Fire

What, you ask, does it mean
To live a Godly life?
It means this one thing:
Lie down in the fire.
Only there, at the fiery heart,
Will you find her.
Only there will you see and taste and know
The flowing being of God,
She in you and you in Her.
Lie down in the fire,
Make it your home
Flow with its flowing
Burn in its burning.

Then, molded together
Fire in fire
Love in love
You will be God with God.

Marguerite Porete
Christian medieval spirituality was much more bodily than ever before
and this was particularly so for women. They knew that bodily
knowing is the beginning of all knowing and this includes the
knowing of God. This is one of the reasons why the Eucharist was so
important to them. There they met the Body of Jesus and absorbed it
sacramentally into their own bodies. Through this bodily encounter,
they came to know their own bodies as the main pathway to God,
and to experience this bodily knowing as something that was eternal
and without beginning or end. The 'four women evangelists' played
a central role in this development. As men struggled with the rational
approach to God and sought Aristotelian understanding of the
'essential' differences between divinity and humanity, thus, in a sense,
alienating themselves from God, the women felt themselves as
mingling in divinity, boundless in their being, and easier able to be a
part of God as their natural habitat, as Mechtilde of Magdeburg had
pointed out.

Marguerite Porete is the supreme example of this new approach to
God, and extremely challenging both to her contemporaries and to
us. Her book, *The Mirror of Simple Souls,* when presented to a team of
theologians was found to be orthodox, but not exactly simple, or for
those of 'simple' faith. What Marguerite intended was that all people,
all 'souls', could have equal access to God, whether they were male or
female, rich or poor, ordained or 'lay'. The notion of the 'laity' was
just then coming into vogue, as clergy were forbidden to marry, and
the extraordinary 'powers' of the priesthood were beginning to be

emphasised. The clergy were the people who 'confected' Christ in the Eucharist and 'forgave' the sins of the non-ordained. But, as the women mystics always taught, direct access to God was available to all, and therefore the mediation of the clergy was not exactly as essential as the Church implied.

Like most medieval women, the early years of Marguerite's life are hidden from us, available only from the occasional biographical references in her book. She seems to have been a highly-educated woman from Hainaut in Northern France. She seems, then, to have been from the nobility, but chose to spend her life as a wandering Beguine teacher. Like other Beguines, she wrote in the vernacular so as to be more available to all, and because of her vernacular theology, she does not cite authorities, but appeals to the 'Book of Experience' as other Beguines did. It is clear, however, that she was familiar with Augustine of Hippo and many other 'authoritative' male theologians, but she chose not to follow them, opting instead to forge her own path to God. We know an enormous amount about the closing years of her life through her trial, imprisonment and execution by burning, simply because the records of the Inquisition are thorough in the extreme.

The Inquisition called Marguerite Porete a 'pseudo-woman' because she did not follow the prescribed path of complementarity for women. She was not submissive, obeyed no male superior, and chose to think and teach and speculate and do theology just as a man would have done. All this was forbidden to women. The reasons for her trial and execution are not clear, despite the abundant records. She is the first case of a woman executed for mystical heresy, but, unfortunately, not the last. She represented the extreme case of the struggle between the mystical life which sought and found a way of direct access to God, and the way of the institutional church which taught that only through the ministrations of the clergy and their mediation could access to God be found. Marguerite said that she had no need of mediation because she was 'oned' with God. And as she continued to teach this to all, her status as a teaching woman came into direct confrontation with the church.

In 1290, Henry of Ghent, a theologian working in Paris, and a contemporary of Marguerite, asked the specific question, 'Can women teach?' and he answered in the negative. Women could not teach in the public forum which belonged to men, but they could teach in private, and, as he added, 'in silence'. This was not the route chosen by Marguerite.

Marguerite Porete wrote her book sometime between 1296 and 1306. As we have said, it was approved by a team of theologians, but after 1308, she was arrested and questioned by the Inquisition. She was given eighteen months to 'consider her position' and during those eighteen months and right up until her death, she maintained total silence as a signal that she did not accept the authority of the Inquisition. She had been handed over to William Humbert, the Dominican Inquisitor in Paris, who condemned her to death after a team of twenty-one theologians examined fifteen propositions from her book. They were declared heretical. We shall look at her teaching later, but the Inquisition feared her freedom of conscience and her utterly profound teaching about the right of all to approach God without fear. She was considered to be quite casual about the ecclesiastical mediation of the clergy, and quite cavalier in her attitude to the 'virtues'. In scholastic theology, the virtues were being enumerated and described and prescribed. Marguerite said they might be necessary for beginners, but eventually, the virtues were just a distraction and made the person focus on themselves rather than on God.

On 1 June 1310, Marguerite Porete was burned at the stake in the Place de Greve in Paris. Her demeanour so impressed the bystanders that many were converted. Her books were also burned, but many survived. Years later, Marguerite's book appeared to great acclaim under the name of a male Carthusian monk, and continued to circulate as his work. It was not until the forties of the last (twentieth) century, that the book was discovered to be Marguerite's and since then it has been studied and acclaimed as a spiritual classic.

Historians are still puzzled by the execution of Marguerite. She doubtless got caught up in the disputes between the King of France and the papacy, but it was primarily because she was a woman who did not fit the prescribed mould and who dared to teach. What did Marguerite teach?

First of all, Marguerite spoke and taught explicitly in her own voice. She did not engage in what has been called the 'rhetoric of diminishment', as did many other women teachers. She did not think or articulate that she was unworthy to speak for God, and that it was really God who was speaking. She spoke in and claimed the authority of her own voice. Likewise, Marguerite did not engage in any of the prescribed exercises of self denial and penances prescribed for women. She felt that she had been made by God in the image of God, the *imago dei*, from all eternity and that therefore she was never removed from God's sight or from God's love. She speaks of knowing God in the place 'where she was before she was' and her goal in life was to return there.

Marguerite aimed to have her teaching made available to all, without exception, but especially to women. The aim of her book is to make reasoning – the main theological activity of the scholastics, as she saw it – dangerous for men, and to show that love was all that was necessary. Just as debates raged about faith and reason, Marguerite, and the other mystics, bypassed the argument to show that love was all that was necessary. Her chosen name for God was Lady Love. Her book, *The Mirror of Simple Souls*, is set out as a dialogue between Lady Love, Reason, the Soul and the 'Far-Nigh', one of her favourite phrases for the Trinitarian God. As Love grows in the soul, the need for Reason dies and the importance of knowing as Love-Knowing develops. She accuses the Church and male theologians of speaking too familiarly and too glibly about God and pretending they know who they are talking about. She calls them 'merchants of God', people who try to contain the mystery of God in 'reasonable' words. For her, the mystery of God is almost incomprehensible, and the soul has to die to itself in order to be united to this mysterious God in love. This 'annihilation' of the soul in God's presence happens towards the end of the human journey, and Marguerite also paints the disappointment and anguish of all those who fear to follow the path of annihilation to the very end. Her mystical theology is apophatic, that is, it is never explanatory, never explicit, but always leaving room for wonder, awe and mystery.

Marguerite wrote that women seem to be able to cross the boundaries between the Divine and the human more easily than the men of her day. Women are less constrained by logic and reason in their dealings with God and seem to be able to flow more freely in and out of humanity and divinity. As we have seen, this 'flowing' metaphor is common to many of the medieval women mystics.

Marguerite Porete regarded the institutional Church of her day with a fairly jaundiced eye. She suggested that there were, in fact, two churches – Holy Church the Great and Holy Church the Less. Holy Church the Less signified the church of reason and Scholastic theology, where men argued about God and tried to contain him in logical definition and reduce God to manageable logic. Holy Church the Great signified the Church of love which was potentially open to everyone and welcomed all those who were trying to love and live by love. This Holy Church the Great was a boundless reality open to all those seeking the mystery of Lady Love. For Marguerite, this was a church for people who sought to 'break through transcendence' and experience a kind of co-naturality with the Divine. Since we have all come from the hand of God, we bear in the depths of our humanity the mark of the Divine, as did Jesus. This means that there is no great gap between humanity and divinity. All are invited to experience this intimacy and identity with God, a sense of resting in the Godhead, a union that is the result of mutual love. As she reflected on this mystery in her beloved Paris, she reflected on the river Seine making its way to the sea and her own and all women's journey towards God:

> Thus she would be like a body of water that flows into the sea, which has some name, as we would say Aisne or Seine. And when this river returns into the sea it loses its course and its name, with which it flows through many countries in accomplishing its task. Now it is the sea where it rests and has lost all labour.

Marguerite's name for this kind of undifferentiated life between God and the human is 'living without a why'. By this she means that we are so essentially one with God as women, even in our God-created bodies, that life is just a question of the unfolding of God's presence, and letting mystery flow from our centre. As she says, 'we have our why within'. This is where Marguerite differs from those spiritual guides who advocate practicing virtue and denying ourselves in order to find God. For her, God was already there in the depths of the self, and it was a question of going within, and not of looking up or out or anywhere else.

As Marguerite describes this journey towards God, she accepts, more or less, the traditional steps on the spiritual journey, at least for beginners: purgation, or the cleansing of the self in preparation for the meeting with God; illumination, the consequent enlightening of the mind and heart after the removal of all sinful tendencies; and union, or the mystical arrival in God's presence. But she utterly rejects all forms of self-denial and self-punishment, and even questions the use of visions and other phenomena on the road to God. Since God is already there in the depths of our being, there is no need for any further search. As other mystics point out, this is so even without baptism, 'just to be born is grace enough'. She never uses visions to support her role as a teacher, but simply accepts her self as a God-inhabited person. And her use of the vernacular also removes her from the aura of clerical authority, where Latin had become the sacred language of divine and human theological discourse.

Marguerite adds some more steps to this spiritual journey, or rather inserts them before the final moment of mystical union. Stage four is 'living without a why', or the realisation that it is God, not us or the virtues or the clergy, who is directing our lives. We experience co-naturality with God, so there is no reason for complicated schemes or methods. Stage five reveals to her the true nature of her inner being, where all the positives that she has built up around her being are brought to nought. This is sometimes called the 'language of unsaying', or the recognition of God's Being as 'No-Thing' and likewise, our own being as 'no-thing'. In this great abyss of love, the darkness is bright with the luminous presence of God and of ourselves in God. What Marguerite is trying to describe here is the notion and mystery of personhood, a notion which had not yet been fully developed. Indeed many authors think that the twelfth century discovered the mystery of person, and indeed the women mystics entered into this discovery with their reflections on the human person of Jesus.

At this stage in the book, Reason cries out, 'I do not understand this', and this leads to the death of Reason. Marguerite is implying that Reason can only go so far, and that it is inadequate for the expression of the mystery of God. This, of course, contradicts much male theology which sees reason and intellect as the main area of likeness to God, a likeness in which only males were created, not females, according to medieval theology. We are now ready to enter stage six, where all mediation ceases, and the oneness of Love is experienced:

> And one sole encounter or one meeting with the ultimate, eternal, ancient and ever-new goodness is more worthy than anything a creature might do, or even the whole Holy Church in a hundred thousand years. God's farness is greater than our nearness.

When this mysterious vacuum is created, the Holy Spirit rushes in to fill the whole space. Now the person has truly become a Mirror, where God sees only God, hence her book's title. In conventional ecclesiastical imagery, seen in the art of many cathedrals, the mirror is the image of the vanity of women, putting on false faces and false personae in order to deceive and entrap lovers. It is the image of vanity. Here, as everywhere in her book, Marguerite overturns such conventional imagery and symbolism in order to reveal the true face of woman, as she saw it. She overturns all the conventional categories of womanhood, which is why the Inquisition named her a *pseudo mulier,* a 'false woman'. It is clear that many of these ecclesiastical attitudes towards women still prevail, as women are excluded from all contributions to church teaching and governance, even on issues that concern their own lives. It is men, and men only, who still write the moral code for women in all aspects of their lives.

Like many of the mystics, Marguerite has a fully-gendered understanding of God. She never tries to internalise the male metaphors for God, or the implications of these for women. Hers is a Christianity without the sin of Eve or the Fall, or the expulsion from God's presence. She always starts from her own experience of God, where, long before she was, she was created by God and never was removed from God's presence. It is a Christianity without original sin or any originating distancing from God. Not that she is unaware of sin, but for her, sin is more a fear of love and following the dictates of love into the loving Presence of God. She sees God's presence in her as a kind of 'internal Scripture' and her task in life is to make this internal Scripture external and reveal it to all in the mystery of true compassion. Marguerite also speaks of the Holy Spirit, writing her book on the 'parchment of her soul' and says that trying to follow the inspiration of the Holy Spirit is like 'trying to capture the sea in her eye'. Her final sense of herself is contained in the marvelous phrase: 'I am who God is through the transformation of love.'

Before we leave these two wonderful Beguine women, it is interesting to note that a recent newspaper report says that the 'world's last Beguine', Marcella Pattyn died on 14 April 2013, aged ninety-two. She had lived since 1941 in the Beguinages at Ghent and Courtrai in Belgium. She was feted by the mayor and townspeople of Courtrai when they realised she was the end of the line in the long and troubled history of the Beguines. A statue was erected in her memory and in memory of all the Beguines who, since the thirteenth century, had preceded her in this distinctly female vocation (*The Economist*, 27 April 2013).

The following pieces attempt to convey the depth and breadth of the spirituality of Marguerite Porete. They contain words and phrases from her brilliant writing and try to reveal the beauty and mystery of her spirituality.

My Name is Joy

God, you call out to me,
And I feel your presence like the great swells of the sea.
My soul swims in this sea of joy and delight,
Which flows and runs from you.
And then, I no longer simply feel joy,
I am joy.
For you, O God,
Lady Joy and Lady Love,
Have transformed me into yourself.
And now, my new name is Joy,
And my new name is Love,
Even though I love so little.
For now
I live by Joy,
And live by Love.

God in the Slaney

Some Sundays
I go looking for God
On the new quays
In old Wexford.

I always have Marguerite in mind.
Look at the Seine, she said,
It rises and takes its travels
Through field, town and forest,
And finally reaches Paris
On its way to the sea.
All the time it is called the Seine,
That is its name.

Then the miracle happens
The Seine reaches the sea
and the Seine loses its own name.
It becomes nameless,
As it mingles
Water with water in the vast moving sea.
And no one can tell
Where the river ends and the sea begins.

And so it is with me, she mused.
I have my own name,
My journey through life,
My travels,
And then, in my seeking,
Like the river,
I enter the vast moving sea of God
And no one can tell
Where I end and God begins.

There I am, God and I,
My nameless self lost
In the vast sea of God's presence,
And who can tell, then,
Where God ends and I begin.

And so, on some Sundays,
I look at the Slaney,
Following its own course
From Lugnaquilla to the sea,
Through Wicklow hills
And Carlow towns,
And Wexford farms
Past Enniscorthy Castle and Cathedrals,
And so on to Wexford,

Where its waters mingle with the sea,
And then it is Slaney no more.

And there, standing on the quay,
I try to see myself, as Marguerite did
Lost and unnamed and mingled in God
Freely swimming in a sea of divinity
Not knowing nor needing to know
Where humanity ends and God begins
Where I end and God begins.

Sometimes then, I turn townward,
With my back to the Slaney-sea
And gaze the length of the quays,
From Crescent Pool,
Past mussel boats,
To the graceful low-slung bridge,
And there
Right in the middle of the quays,
I try to imagine a woman
Being burned to death
On the Wexford quays
Just as Marguerite was
Right there in the middle of the Place de Greve
In her beloved Paris
On the first day of June
In the year thirteen-ten.

How to imagine such a horror,
How to imagine the fear that one lone woman
Could evoke in the fierce, fiery fear-filled church.

Was it because she spoke of swimming in divinity?
Was it because her chosen name for her God

Was Lady-Love?
Was it because, as a woman,
She dared to teach about her woman-God of love?

How could they have been so terrified
Of this one woman, Marguerite,
Whose calm acceptance of her horrific death
Silenced the onlookers into awed reverence?

That day, the Seine provided no answers,
And today, turning again towards the sea-bound Slaney,
I seek, not answers,
But some small share of her God-lost self,
Some sense of her all-embracing briny divinity,
Some feeling that here,
In Wexford between Slaney and sea,
I will learn to keep looking
And not miss the great moments of mingling.

Lone Mystics

It is the Second Creation Story, the story of Adam and Eve, that has dominated the theology of the Christian Church. The story of the Fall, the deception of Eve, original sin and the Redemption have formed the bedrock of Christian teaching. As is obvious, this cannot be the starting point for women, who do not experience themselves as responsible for all the ills of the human race. It was primarily, but not only, in the writings of Marguerite Porete that women began to pay attention to the First Creation Story and their experience of being created in the image of God as women and not as pseudo men. So Creation was their starting point. They did not experience a great gap of sinfulness between God and themselves, but saw themselves as coming straight from the creating hands of God, in whose image they were made. And it was very good. They reached towards intimacy and even identity with this God, and the way was opened for them through the life of Jesus, his human life. They understood that they shared this humanity. For them, therefore, humanity and divinity were not strangers, but intimately linked with each other. This is all the more remarkable given the unbroken official tradition of teaching about women as daughters of Eve, which was even more persistent and divisive in the Middle Ages, even to the point of outright misogyny.

It is this experience of intimacy that marks all the women mystics, and shines out in the lives of the two women we shall explore in this chapter, Julian of Norwich and Catherine of Siena. These two women did not have the protection of a religious order, or even of a Beguine community. They were lone mystics, therefore more vulnerable to the wrath of the church towards women who stepped out of line. The condemnation and destruction of the Beguine movement had taken place in the early-fourteenth century, so these two women had to tread a more careful path. Executions by fire of women and other 'heretics' were taking place almost daily. The church was no longer tolerant in any way of these women and most women had been terrorised into silence. The dreadful 'witch-craze' – the burning of women as witches, was picking up speed and the fear and horror of 'false' women and 'wicked' women was widespread, and, it seems, deliberately spread by the Church. Besides, the great plague of the early-fourteenth century had terrified people. Almost one-third of Europe was dead and the wrath of God wielding havoc on the people was on the mind of everyone.

It was into the end stage of this period that both Julian and Catherine were born. There is a new sense of caution in their writing as they try to express their discoveries about God in the context of a fearful male-dominated church. This did not keep them from expressing their delight and astonishment at the closeness of God and God's generosity towards all, but in the context of the time, their courage is remarkable.

Julian of Norwich

Like so many other women of history, much of our knowledge of Julian is a kind of guess work, gleaned from the pages of her book, *Revelations of Divine Love,* or *The Showings,* as Julian herself liked to call it. Her glowing personality shines through on every page, but biographically, the details are scant.

One precise date is noted and made the focus of Julian's whole life. On 8 May 1373, when she was thirty years of age, and close to death after being anointed by her local priest, who held a crucifix before her eyes, Julian experienced her sixteen *Showings.* She immediately recovered, to the joy of her grieving mother, and began to write down the details of the visions. Twenty years later, after decades of prayer and reflection, Julian wrote a longer version of this experience. Both these versions survive as the *Short Text* and the *Long Text*. This longer text, in particular, has become one of the best known of women's mystical texts, with the famous quotation, 'All shall be well, and all shall be well and all manner of thing shall be well' on almost everyone's lips.

Julian tells us that she considered the sixteen visions to be an answer to a threefold prayer she had made earlier in life, asking for 'the mind of the Passion', as Mary, the mother of Jesus and Mary Magdalene might have experienced it; for a severe illness early in life, so that on recovery she might have a second chance in her search for God; and for the 'wounds' of contrition, compassion and longing for God. These three prayers, and what she understood as the response to them, formed the basis of her life and prayer until she died, probably around 1416. Her own testimony of the date of her visions tells us that she was born in 1342. There are two other contemporary references to her life. One reference is in the autobiography of Margery Kempe, an extraordinary woman from nearby King's Lynn, who also experienced divine revelations and went to the more famous Julian for reassurance and encouragement. She tells us that she was delighted with her visit. Two more dissimilar personalities are hard to imagine. Julian comes across as calm and dignified. Margery was always rambunctious, seeking attention and vocally claiming her place as one of God's chosen. A final reference to Julian's life appears in two wills from the early fifteenth century that mention her as a beneficiary.

Sometime in her early thirties, Julian became a recluse at the Church of St Julian, from which her name is derived. The infamous Bishop of Norwich, Bishop Despenser, performed the ceremony of enclosure. With this vicious and murderous man as one's bishop, one can understand why Julian had to tread carefully. We know nothing of Julian's early life, her education, her family or the influences on her early spiritual development. We don't even know her real name. It is safe to assume that, since her writing on the motherhood of God forms one of the central themes of her mystical life, her own mother was a caring and compassionate woman.

Julian lived at an extraordinary time. The Hundred Years War was waging between France and England (and most of Europe). The Black Death reached Norwich in 1348, when Julian was a child, and killed one-third of the population of the town. During most of her lifetime, the papacy was in exile in Avignon (1309–1378), and on the conclusion of this exile, the Great Western Schism took place when two and then three popes disputed the papacy (1378–1417). The peasant revolt under Wat Tyler also took place and the leaders were executed by Julian's bishop. It was this same war-like bishop, Bishop Despenser, who was called to lead the Crusade that Catherine of Siena and Popes Gregory and Urban had continually called for. Participation in the Crusade offered remission of all sins of all relatives who had died in the Black Plague, and occasioned wild enthusiasm. And finally John Wycliff, the founder and leader of the Lollards, a 'heretical' English group, harbinger of the Protestant Reformation, who wanted all, women and men to study the Bible among other things, flourished around Norwich during Julian's lifetime. Many of the Lollards were later executed by Bishop Despenser in the Lollard Pit around the corner from Julian's hermitage. She could not have failed to smell the burning bodies. Also in Julian's lifetime, the first English language bible was published in 1390.

Not one whit of any of this penetrates the calm atmosphere of Julian's hermitage, even though it was situated right on one of the main thoroughfares of Norwich, where all traffic to the Continent had to pass. The hermitage was set up in such a way that one window looked onto the church, so Julian could attend all the services, and one window looked on to the town, so she could receive visitors, alms, counsel people and receive requests for prayers. The literature of the time warns hermits not to dally at this window and get distracted from their main task which was prayer.

Julian's whole life in the hermitage was taken up with trying to understand the meaning of her visions, which, like Catherine later, were focused on the Passion. This was not only centred on the sufferings, but on the fact that this was the core of the humanity of Jesus. We hear of no account of any penitential activity in Julian's life, nor did she recommend such to others. For Julian, as for all medieval women mystics, her main focus was on the Trinity and on the marvelous interlinking of humanity and divinity. For Julian, there was no distancing of God, who was 'closer than hands and feet'. From her reflections, she worked out a whole theology, which was named by Thomas Merton as the most appropriate theology for the twentieth century.

Julian constantly affirms her orthodoxy and her fidelity to Holy Mother Church, but she also struggles to reconcile the teaching of her visions with the teaching of the Church. For example, she says, 'Holy Church taught me that sinners are worthy of blame and wrath, but in my showings, there was no wrath in God.' This was an extraordinary insight at the time, when the whole world was shuddering at the wrath of God, demonstrated, as they thought, in the Plague and the other calamities of the time. Julian was almost contemporary in her understanding of God's justice. Traditionally it has been understood as the right of God to mete out rewards and punishment. For Julian, there is no punishment from God – this is the context of her most famous saying that 'all will be well'.

Julian wanted her life to be of lasting significance, especially in the communication of this truth. She wanted, like so many other women mystics, to focus only on love. Love is essential to human wholeness, and the task of the Christian is to negotiate the journey to full humanity, in imitation of Jesus. This is a journey of love. Because of her insistence on human wholeness through love, Julian has been called the 'theologian of integration'. Julian has little room for sin, which she describes as simply forgetting who we are before God, and giving in to self-doubt. Her images are always of restored relationships, healing, recreating ourselves, struggling with our broken hearts because of the injustice of the world, and open and public compassion for all.

'Holy Church teaches me to believe that there are people in hell,' she says. But she simply cannot accept this, because of the mystery of

God's marvelous Creation, and the mingling of humanity and divinity in every human person. She learned from her visions and teaches that we are composed of a divine substance, which can never be touched or damaged or destroyed. And we are composed of what she calls 'sensuality' which we share with the humanity of Jesus. It is noteworthy that most other theologians of the time taught that we share this sensuality with the animals. This demonstrates the extraordinary innovation of Julian's theology, which, as we know well, was never accepted by the Church. Her inability to believe in hell is probably the reason why she has never been canonised or made a doctor of the church.

This is one of the central struggles of Julian's life and she constantly returns to God in her prayer to try to deal with it. God's response to her was that 'all shall be well, and all manner of thing shall be well'. And Julian enlarged on this by telling her famous parable of 'The Lord and the Servant'. This was a story about a servant who joyfully and eagerly went off to do his Lord's bidding, but along the way fell into a ditch and could not get out. Then he fell into despair about his own worthlessness, his inability to do his master's bidding, and the supposed anger of the Lord at this failure. But, according to Julian, that was not the story at all. The Lord loved his servant, felt only compassion for him and never stopped loving him. It was the servant who misunderstood the whole situation. It is this emphasis on God's never-ending love, which makes Julian's writing stand out from that of all other theologians, past and present.

Julian's idea of Creation is summed up in the brilliant parable of the hazelnut:

And God showed me something small, no bigger than a hazelnut lying in the palm of my hand, and I perceived that it was round as any ball. I looked at it and thought: What can this be? And I was given the general answer: It is everything that is made. I was amazed that it could last, for I thought that it was so little that it could suddenly fall into nothing. And I was answered in my understanding: it lasts and always will because God loves it; and thus everything has being through the love of God.

And she added, 'God is everything that is good and the goodness that everything has is God.'

Julian looked out at the world from her hermitage and saw only the love of God and the potential for goodness and therefore godliness in every human being. She saw that this all came about through the humanity of Jesus, and through that humanity, we all can learn how to be human. Julian, like many other mystics, does not need Jesus as Redeemer, because she does not perceive that human beings are separated from God. There is no gap to be bridged, no original sin to be atoned. Jesus brought out for us the real meaning of humanity, and each one of us can learn the depths of this humanity in our own lives.

As Julian described this humanity, it appeared to her that she needed more in her understanding of God than the male dominant imagery which she, like all Christians, had inherited, And so, more than any other medieval theologian, she worked out her thinking on God – and Jesus – as Mother. 'Our substance is our Mother, God all Wisdom,' she said, as she begins her reflection in the *Long Text*. Twenty years of reflection on her earlier encounter with God had brought her to this conviction of God as Mother, the only way she could think of to delineate what she had discovered about the Being and Goodness of God. 'Jesus is our mother, in whom we are endlessly born,' she wrote, again naming a quality she had discovered in Jesus that was absent from all official theology. She tells us that God further showed her: 'This I am, the capability and goodness of the Fatherhood. This I am, the wisdom of the Motherhood. This I am, the light and grace that is all love.' Her reflection on her own mother doubtless influenced her thoughts on the motherhood of God. 'A mother's service is nearest, readiest and surest. This office no one can do or know, or ever will do fully, but God alone.' And she added, the human person that is born from this Mother God, that follows in the footsteps of Jesus, the Mother, is substantially united with God. The whole of faith, she explains, is nothing but a right understanding of who we are, a right understanding 'that we are in God and God is in us'.

Julian does not deny the existence of sin but sees it as secondary and also necessary. Sin arises from a lack of self-worth, forgetting who we are and who God is. Our sin reveals to us the endlessness of God's care for us, and the reality of the substance of God in the core of our being. Julian's theology and anthropology do not admit any dualisms. Everything is 'oned with God' through the humanity of Jesus. Like the hazelnut, the whole world is one, safe in the hands of a God who is both Mother and Father. The traditional imagery of the spiritual life depicted a ladder, up which we climbed from this arena of sin towards the goodness and purity of God. Julian never uses this image, but depicts the spiritual life as a journey of unfolding the presence of God which has been there from the very beginning and has never been lost. Her favourite words to describe our relationship with God are 'unfolding', 'embracing', 'digging' and 'discovery'.

How can we sum up the theology of Julian of Norwich? It is a six-fold theological gift from her cell in Norwich to the modern world. Julian lived in a pre-Reformation and entirely patriarchal Church, but she was able to see beyond the present deformities to a more inclusive Church through the humanity of Jesus.

God is to be found wherever there is goodness and love. Julian moves away from the scholastic emphasis on being and reason, and therefore on orthodox thinking. Julian is a profound thinker but only on the meaning of love.

There is no body/soul dualism, no 'between', no gaps between God and us. As human beings, we have a 'noble making' and the 'body and soul form a glorious union'. She totally moves away from the teaching of Augustine of Hippo that the body is always at war with the soul. She even questions the use that other theologians make of the word 'soul'. For her, 'soul' is never a substance apart from our bodiliness.

Our sensuality can rightly be called our soul. All is oned with God. In God our sensuality and substance are one. Our sensuality is the mystery of the Incarnation through which we are oned with God.

Our senses, she tells us, reveal God to us. We see, hear, taste, feel and breathe in God at all times.

The whole aim of salvation is to make us one with God. The Passion is the great act of 'oneing' us. The coming of Jesus was like a second creation. Now, God is in everything we do, even the most mundane thing, like using the bathroom, she points out. This is God working in us and through us.

The Motherhood of God and Jesus is where we were created. 'The whole property of Motherhood is found in the Trinity.' This theology of motherhood is quite astonishing. It reveals in that one word what theology might have been like, had women been given their voice from the beginning. For Julian, the woman theologian, motherhood is the best image possible for describing the experience of being 'enclosed' by God. Her language of God is always about an enveloping embrace, the curvature of God. Motherhood, for her, is also the best image of compassion. God is motherhood at work. Birthing is the great work of motherhood in pain and struggle. This is what the Passion signified to Julian. Jesus gave birth to us. God gives birth to the whole of creation. Creation is the first birthing. It is interesting, in this ecological era, when the Big Bang is in common parlance the starting point of creation (and even the name of a popular television programme) that the gentler image of the birthing of creation came to Julian long before the opening up of physics and astronomy.

Humanity has been divinised. 'We are of God.' Julian says over and over again that she sees no difference between God and our substance. 'God is God and we are in God.'

God never began to love us. 'And I saw no wrath in God.' God's love is courteous and homely. We are loved whether we are noble or lowly. 'In our creation, we were knitted and oned with God.' This love of God for us and our love for God naturally leads to a life of service. God serves the whole of creation in love. So do we, as we love and serve in our part of creation.

The hopeful, almost cheerful theology of Julian is a total contrast to her contemporaries, who were still floundering in the tragedy of the Great Plague and the sense that this was an angry God's punishment on the human race. Julian does not mention outside conditions, but her God did not know anger, did not condemn humans, no matter how 'sinful' and did not stand at a distance from the earth.

The following pieces give some indication of Julian's profound sense of intimacy with this God.

Love is What God is

Would you know God's meaning in this thing?
Learn it well;
Love is God's meaning.
Who showed this to you?
Love.
What did God show you?
Love.
Why did God show it to you?
For love.
And I saw surely that before God made us,
God loved us.
And this love has never slackened
And never will.
And in this love,
God has done everything.
And in this love,
God has made all things profitable for us.
And in this love,
Our life is everlasting.

Seeking is Seeing

Seeking God is as good as seeing God.
Who, but a saint,
Would know so clearly
That the journey is the reality,
The steps are sight,
The effort is reward,
The seeing is the searching,
The dream is the reality?
Seeking God is seeing God.

A God Who Gives

God of love and life,
The pattern of your presence among us is clear enough:
You give and we receive.
You give with overwhelming generosity,
And we receive with our customary casualness.
You give more then we can ask or imagine,
And we receive, sometimes in wonder.

You give us life and breath, and we receive,
You give miracles of newness, and we receive.
You give rain and sunshine and food, and we receive.
You give yourself in prophetic voice,
And in the most unexpected holy people, and we receive,
You take and bless and break and give, and we receive.

But sometimes you challenge us in overwhelming mystery
And awesome destruction.
The world shakes on its foundation and we are terrified.

The waters move beyond their bounds and we feel engulfed.
The mountains crush the valleys
And we cry from the buried depths.

Do not, we pray, allow our hearts to go numb
When this happens.
Do not, we beg, allow us to give in to tempting paralysis.
Move us, in those times of dread,
To take our turn as the givers,
So that all may find food and shelter and care and nourishment.
Open our hearts to hear the cries of those who weep,
So that what we have received from you in abundance,
May be passed on to all.
Help us, O God who is Love,
And O Love who is God,
To love, even in our own faltering way.

God of Life and Love,
The pattern of your presence among us is clear:
You give and we receive;
You challenge and we are afraid.
Be with us as we learn again to see you in the giving and receiving,
The generosity and the fear,
The alarm and the hope.
And let us learn to repeat with the psalmist:
God is our refuge and strength, a very present help in trouble.
(Psalm 46:1)

Catherine of Siena (1347–1380)
Catherine of Siena, Doctor of the Church, is one of the most extraordinary women and extraordinary people in the history of the

Church. She is at once humane and manic, delightfully unpretentious and sometimes almost hysterical in her attitude to things divine. She was profoundly committed to the Church of her day, with all its failings and even corruption, and radically anti-Church, almost unknowingly, in her utterly independent attitude to her own following of God. As with all mystics, she 'obeyed God rather than man', but also clung to obedience to a pope whom a good part of the rest of the Church considered to be an anti-pope. Catherine lived during one of the most confusing times in the history of the Church, with the papacy in Avignon for most of her life and then descending into the farce of the Great Western Schism, in her final years. Besides this, she survived the Great Plague, as her twin sister did not, and though reclusive and alone, in the sense that she was not part of any official religious community of nuns, involved herself totally and very publicly in the affairs of the Church. Unlike Julian of Norwich, Catherine was a mystic on the move, from Siena to Avignon to Florence to Rome, repeatedly, in her efforts to pull the Church back from the brink, and most of this labour was when she was in her twenties.

Catherine and her twin were the twenty-fourth and twenty-fifth children of their mother, Mona Lappa, and father, a well-known Sienese businessman. She was born in 1347, just as the plague was at its height in Siena. From the very beginning, Catherine showed an intense streak of independence, resisted all efforts to marry her off to save the family fortune, and throughout her teens, spent her life in total isolation in her room in prayer and penance. This was partly a family punishment for what they saw as her wilfulness, partly Catherine's own choice. At the age of eighteen, she joined the Mantellate, a kind of Dominican third Order for widows, but Catherine never took the vows of Religious Life. This was in response to what she claimed as a divine vision bidding her to go downstairs and dine with her family, and start going out into the wider world.

At the age of twenty-one, Catherine experienced what she described as a mystical marriage, and this experience launched her on her public career as teacher, reformer, director, preacher, healer and friend to all.

It is clear that, in the absence of ordination or any other ecclesiastical approbation, Catherine and many other mystics needed just such a divine launching pad, in order to enter public life as a preacher and teacher. Soon, Catherine was joined by a group of women and men who were named, sometimes derisively as *Caterinati,* and who remained as her closest companions for the remainder of her life. This group was totally engaged in the reform of the Church of their day, above all, the process of returning the pope to Rome from Avignon. As part of this reform. Catherine, together with the pope, urgently preached the necessity of a new Crusade to rid the Church totally of its corrupting elements. This Crusade was to be led by the Bishop of Norwich, who exercised such a violent influence on Julian's home Church community.

Around 1374, Catherine began her intense period of travel and activity for the reform of the Church. By now, her fame had spread all over Europe, particularly as a mediator in difficult family and city feuds. At the age of twenty-seven, Catherine undertook her first journey to Florence, where she nursed people through another bout of plague. While the pope and his court were detained in Avignon, many of the cities of Italy united against the papacy in the Tuscan League. Florence was put under interdict or excommunication and eventually the Florentines asked Catherine to travel to Avignon to ask Pope Gregory XI to cancel this interdict. It was around this time that Catherine began her letter-writing campaign to all and sundry in her intense efforts to win support for the pope in his absence, and also to persuade the pope himself to bestir himself and return to Rome. We have about four hundred of her letters, and they reveal a quick, plain-speaking and intensely committed mind which brooked no refusal of her requests. So in 1376–77, Catherine and her little band of followers, set out from Siena to Avignon to meet the pope personally and plead on behalf of the Florentines.

Pope Gregory eventually returned to Rome in 1377 and Catherine returned to Siena, where she set about writing her great mystical treatise, *The Dialogue.* This was when, at the age of thirty, Catherine learned to write herself, instead of using a secretary. It is said that she had kept several secretaries going all at the same time, as she was writing her letters. In 1378, Catherine seems to have organised a women's monastic community for some of her followers and that same year, Pope Gregory died and was replaced by Pope Urban VI. This was one of the most disastrous choices possible, as Urban had a violent and completely uncontrolled temper. As a result, the same group of cardinals elected Clement as pope and initiated one of the worst ecclesiastical crises, with two popes and the resulting Church schism. Countries, kings, abbots and bishops lined up behind their chosen pope and the Church fell into total chaos. The new pope, Urban, summoned Catherine to Rome in an attempt to gain support for his cause. Shortly thereafter, Catherine suffered a stroke and died in Rome at the age of thirty-three.

One of the extraordinary aspects of Catherine's life was her inability to eat. This *inedia* has a very contemporary aspect in *anorexia nervosa* and its many associated eating disorders. Throughout her life, Catherine tried to eat but was unable to bring herself to consume anything other than a very small amount of raw vegetables. Even though, unlike many other women mystics, Catherine was a child of her time in her belief in a penitential life, her *inedia* went beyond this. Some suggest that it was a deep psychological reaction to the death of her twin sister as a baby. This infant had been sent to a wet nurse and died. Catherine was nursed by her mother and lived. This was also at the height of the plague in Siena, so the explanation of her infant sister's death could be obvious. Nevertheless, there is also some suggestion that Catherine's mother, in her early rages at Catherine's refusal to marry suggested that the wrong twin survived. Apocryphal or not, this tale has a human ring to it and may have influenced Catherine. Nevertheless, whatever the reason, it is fairly clear that Catherine died partly of self-starvation.

As was mentioned, Catherine was a woman of her times. Unlike Julian of Norwich in her cell, Catherine was intensely and consistently involved in the life of the Church. It was a restless and feverish concern for the good of the Church at every level. She seemed to have spent her time badgering everyone from pope to prince to work for reform and the glory of God, with hardly any signs of success. Her theology and much of her spirituality were in line with the conventions of the time. Unlike Julian, again, Catherine believed in and needed an angry God to punish all those working against the Church. She believed in hell and in a God who sent people into hell-fire, again, quite understandably but quite unlike Julian. Catherine's goals for most of her very short life were four-fold: to bring the pope back to Rome and thus prevent the unseemly and violent wrangling among the Italian cities; to persuade the pope to forgive the people of Florence and cancel the interdict against them; to have the pope inaugurate another Crusade against heretics and infidels; and finally, and perhaps most important of all, to engage in a vast reform of the clergy.

On the other hand, Catherine was a woman totally outside her time and radically involved in a spirituality that would be influential for centuries. She was driven by a restless desire for God. Indeed, the first words of her *Dialogue* are, 'A soul rises up, restless with tremendous desire for God's honour and the salvation of souls.' She insisted all through her life on finding a space for prayer, for mysticism, in the worst possible surroundings, to such an extent that she made the mystical life her whole personality. In the midst of this intensely lived life of reform, Catherine was a brilliant, warm and loving giver and receiver of friendship. For her, friendship was an experience of heaven, and the lack of friends a foretaste of hell. She said that she learned everything she knew from 'conversation' with her friends about God, and 'devouring their faces' in an effort to get close to their deepest thoughts. Despite the fact that she was rarely alone, prayer was the integrating factor in her life. This small, feverish, almost manic woman, driven by her enormous energy and restless desire for God, held huge influence over popes, cities and the whole Church of God.

One of the hallmarks of Catherine's spirituality was a constant thirst for self-knowledge. She spoke constantly of entering into the 'cell of self-knowledge', because there she discovered God and the goodness of God in her own life. This self-knowledge, she said, precedes love, and it is in these two areas that her friends were so important to her. Love always leads to truth, and Catherine spoke frequently of 'clothing herself' in truth. She who was wasting away from lack of food, spoke of 'growing so fat on the love of God, that her clothes were bursting'.

For Catherine, it was the Holy Spirit who opened the door to self-knowledge at Pentecost, and it was Christ who led the way in this feast of knowing and loving. Jesus is the Bridge (one of her favourite images), uniting humanity and divinity, and it is in this sense of the intimacy of humanity and divinity – even woman's humanity – that Catherine joins with the agenda of the other women mystics. 'The divinity is kneaded into our very being just like a loaf of bread,' she says in one of her many down-to-earth images. She speaks of the three stages of the spiritual life as starting from the feet, when we walk away from sin, going towards the heart where we know the love of God partly through the love of our friend, and then to the mouth where we learn to experience the taste of peace.

Catherine was intensely focused on the Crucifixion of Jesus, not necessarily the suffering, but the attitude and deep being of Jesus in this extraordinary act. Almost like Julian, when she speaks of the teaching of Jesus, she means what we can learn from the Cross. She rarely speaks of the parables and miracles of Jesus, or of his actual words. It is a process of learning from utter love for us, for the world, for all. She learned from God in her prayer, she tells us, that Jesus is the whole of God's truth.

Catherine's sense of herself before God was similar to that of many of the other women mystics, a sense of deep intimacy, even of identity between humanity and divinity. She tells us that she learned from God – and this is part of her self-knowledge – that 'the greatest sin is not to see Me in yourself'. If we do not experience God's intimate presence like this, it means that 'we are sailing with the wrong wind'. But when we sail with the right wind, God tells her that 'he makes of her another himself', and says, 'you are another me'. Despite Catherine's sense of evil, corruption and sin in the Church and in the world, in her own life, she seems to have rooted the sense of herself, as other women mystics did, in the First Creation Story and her creation in the image of God. This was an utterly felt reality for her. 'I made you in my image and now I have taken on your image,' and as Catherine says, 'then in the gentle mirror of God, I saw my own dignity'.

In this world of endless activity, travel, mediation and contention, it is astonishing that Catherine places so much emphasis on friendship. She tells us that we love God because there is a commandment to do so, but with our friends, we experience a 'free exchange of love', which must be the kind of love that God feels in the trinity and for us. Catherine's friends included women and men, priests and nuns, princes and paupers. As their friend, she accuses some of her wealthy companions of giving into greed, which makes them arrogant and dishonest, so that 'instead of sharing with the poor, you steal from them'. 'True friends', she says, 'are drawn together like the two natures of Christ', into one total loving union.

Perhaps the last words about Catherine are best left to the one she describes as the Devil, who said this to her; 'Damnable woman, there is no getting at you. You have beaten me with humility and the cudgel of charity'.

Our Special Friends

We love everyone with a generous love,
But God sometimes gives us also a special love
To love more intimately one person,
Who then becomes a close particular friend.
This is so that we can support each other more faithfully,
For the love with which I love myself,
That is the love with which I love my friend.

This is how it is with very dear friends:
Their loving affection makes them two bodies with one soul,
Because love transforms us into what we love.
And if these souls are made one
Nothing can be hidden from them,
Don't let cowardice keep you from loving.

But even more,
God has so identified with us
That our love for one another truly binds us to God as well.
Jesus told me:
'I have put you among others
So that you can do for them what you cannot do for me.
Love them without any concern for thanks,
And without looking for any profit for yourself,
And whatever you do for them,
I will consider done to me.'

Women and Missions

The calamitous fourteenth century, as it has been called, was devastated by the bubonic plague mid-century and several lesser outbreaks of plague throughout the remaining years. The continent of Europe lost about one-third of its population and the survivors were left in a state of intense fear and a sense of hopelessness. For Christian Europe, it seemed that God had definitely turned his back on a sinful people. On the human level, a search for human scapegoats took place and one of the results was an upsurge in the misogyny that had reached a peak in the High Middle Ages, with the emphasis on clerical celibacy. We know that celibacy was almost universally ignored, in practice, but preachers and teachers pointed to women as the main enemies of a priestly celibate life. A wave of witch-burnings was the result as rulers, both lay and clerical, tried to regain control of their domains, and root out the all too evident works of the devil. Belief in witchcraft and the vicious presence of witches became part of the official doctrine of the Christian Church.

As the world recovered its equilibrium throughout the fifteenth century, a remarkable literary quarrel broke out in the midst of wars and continuing devastation for most people. It was called la *querelle des femmes*, a continuous literary diatribe against women. The difference this time was that one remarkable woman plucked up her pen to respond to the scurrilous accusations against women. Her name was Christine de Pisan. Because of family tragedies, she was left in her twenties to be the breadwinner for her family and she chose writing as her occupation of choice. As far as we know, she was the first woman to earn her living by the pen. One of her main works, *The City of Ladies,* tackles the hoary old complaints about women, and for the first time, puts down on paper what a female response might be. In her time she gained notoriety, but her name and her work have survived the travails of the fifteenth century. Most unusually for women, Christine was able to see herself in the context of her time and in the context of history. She was a gifted philosopher and she was able to point out the inequities and inaccuracies of the usual anti-women diatribes. Christine was the first woman to indicate that the first task of a woman trying to live an independent life was to prove that she was human and that as a human being she had the capacity to think, to reason and to do philosophy and theology. This was a remarkable public stance to take, given the fact that these obvious womanly traits are not as yet recognised in the Catholic Church of the twenty-first century.

As far as the Christian Church was concerned, the fifteenth century saw a succession of the most gifted and some of the most corrupt popes the church had ever seen. Pope Sixtus IV (1471–1484) was a warlike and amazingly greedy pope who promoted the Spanish and Roman inquisitions with great enthusiasm and directed his soldiers in their defense of and advance of the Papal territories. These vast military engagements needed endless supplies of money, and it was Sixtus, apparently, who first came up with the idea of offering indulgences for the dead at a price. When this offer was accompanied with the most lurid account of the pains of purgatory, the money rolled in. Together with his successors, Innocent VIII (1484–1492) and the Borgia pope, Alexander VI (1492–1503), decrees were issued against Jews and Muslims, offering only forced conversions or death. Alexander was known as a murderer and adulterer before he became pope and his character did not improve in the papacy. These men were reported to have lowered the moral tone of the whole continent, and cries for reform began to be heard from many quarters, as the Church seemed to be intent on destroying itself.

In the midst of all this, one of the most corrupt periods in the history of the Church, Martin Luther (1483–1546) grew to manhood, as well as the great theologian and reformer, Erasmus of Rotterdam (1467–1536). Erasmus saw clearly that the Scriptures had been all but forgotten in the Church of his day and he devoted his life and his abundant writings to remedying this situation. His was only one of the most scholarly and vocal cries for reform. As we know, Martin Luther finally ran out of patience with the wholesale merchandising of indulgences and in October 1517, he famously nailed his Ninety-Five Theses for reform to the door of Wittenberg Cathedral. It is only in retrospect that this event assumes such great significance. At the time, it caused barely a ripple in Rome and was treated as a local, minor incident. But Martin Luther had read the temper of the times better than any pope, and within a few decades, the Christian Church had been divided irreparably.

This is not the place to detail the history of the multiple reformations that followed on Martin Luther's initial protest, but to set the scene for the next moment of women's 'intrusion' into the affairs of the men's Church. Eventually the cries for reform reached the ears of Pope Paul III (1534–1549) and quite reluctantly, an Ecumenical Council was summoned to take place in the then German city of Trent. Paul III may have been some improvement on fifteenth-century popes but he resisted calls for reform strenuously. He himself had four children and spent a good part of his papacy trying to enrich his family, principally by making his 'nephews' cardinals, some from the age of twelve. Since the great Western Schism in the mid-fifteenth century when three popes tried to govern the Church simultaneously, and the Council of Constance that ended that schism, a fear of councils had entered the papal consciousness. The Council of Constance had called for the reform of the Church in 'head and members' and there ensued multiple debates about the relative powers of pope and council. With the calling of the Council of Trent in 1545, Pope Paul knew that he was opening himself and his curia to many challenges. He resisted conciliar attempts at reform of the papacy with all his might and tried to reserve to himself alone, the reform of the papacy and cardinals.

There is a huge gap between the actual Council of Trent, which was a fairly shambolic event and the eventual Tridentine reform which gave birth to the Roman Catholic Church and its rigidly doctrinal traditions which prevailed for the next three hundred years.

It is easy to forget now that the bishops then needed their rulers' permission to attend the council and this partly explains the fact – the other reason was apathy and resistance – that only twenty-nine bishops, out of a possible seven hundred, were present for the opening sessions. Despite many internal disputes about who would set the agenda for the Council, it was actually Martin Luther's agenda. A decision was eventually made to run a parallel stream of doctrinal and ecclesiastical reform, one succeeding the other. The Council eventually sat over eighteen years, from 1545 to 1563, with three sessions. By the end of the first session, it was obvious that reconciliation with the Protestants was now impossible, and the Council set about reforming the Church internally. Doctrinally, the main focus was on Luther's teaching of justification by faith alone and the theology and institution of the seven sacraments. On the reform agenda was the effort to have one bishop actually residing in each diocese and one priest actually residing in his parish, with the goal of both bishop and priest to engage in the pastoral care of their people. This, of course, meant for both priest and bishop, the relinquishing of the multiple benefices that served only to fill their coffers.

Again, this is not the place to cover the history of the Council of Trent, but to point out its most significant decisions for the future of the Roman Catholic Church. From the doctrinal point of view, the emphasis on the personal institution of the seven sacraments by Jesus Christ, and the re-emphasis on the doctrine of original sin were primary. One of the main additions to these already fairly traditional doctrines was the emphasis on the presence of the priest as witness at the Sacrament of Matrimony. This was an attempt, eventually very successful, to wipe out clandestine or private marriages and make divorce impossible for Catholics. Another detail which marked the Church for centuries was the introduction of confession boxes for the Sacrament of Penance.

On the reform front, and also part of the reorganisation of the Sacrament of Holy Orders, was the institution of diocesan seminaries with an established curriculum to counter the presence of so many ignorant and often illiterate clergy.

The Council was hampered by endless warfare between nations and the Holy Roman Empire, and between the emperor and the pope. Often there were no French bishops present, at other times no German bishops, and all along the line papal interference hampered the Council's work.

In the church at large, as we have said, there were many cries for reform, but the Council of Trent might have remained a dead letter, were it not for the actual reform movements that were already functioning in the Church. These included the reformed Carmel of Teresa of Avila, the new Jesuit educational and missionary work of Ignatius of Loyola's Jesuits, and the actual work of education and healing on the ground, of a growing number of women's religious orders, starting with the Ursulines and the English Ladies of Mary Ward, better known today as the Loreto Sisters.

In retrospect, it is quite extraordinary that the Council of Trent had no interest whatsoever in either missions or women, at a time when the roles of women were being actively discussed in both Renaissance and Reform circles, and also at a time when the cosy European world was being blown wide open by Spanish and Portuguese explorers. The Council of Trent was explicitly male and Eurocentric. The only mention of women was to reaffirm the rule of cloister for all religious women, which was added to the decrees on almost the last day. This one decree caused more heartache to later women founders of religious communities than almost any other aspect of the Council.

Teresa of Avila and the Carmelite Reform

Theoretically Teresa of Avila (1515–1582) lived in a cloistered Carmelite monastery, but her travels brought her the length and breadth of Spain, to the extent that her enemies, and they were plenty, called her a 'gadabout woman'. This was, perhaps, one of the worst slurs on women, who were supposed to be either cloistered or confined to their private quarters under the control of their husbands. Like other great reforming Christian teachers of the era, Teresa's solution to the devastation of Church life was the virtue of obedience, which was central to her monastic reform, but she herself seems not really to have obeyed anyone in her life. As later commentators would remark on other women founders, they covered their disobedience under the cloak of obedience. The fact is that if she – and other women founders – had not disobeyed, their endeavours would never have seen the light of day.

Spain in the sixteenth century was one of the greatest world powers. It was an intensely Catholic country, with a very active inquisition which aimed to stamp out all heresy from the country, including Jews and Muslims. Spain was also engaged in world conquest and the 'discovery' of the New World of the Americas opened the doors to unimaginable riches and also a new harvest of souls. These new converts would replace the loss to the Catholic Church of the Protestant Reform communities who were by mid-century well established across Northern Europe. The founding of the Jesuits by Ignatius Loyola (1491–1556) gave the church an Order of priests whose motto was also obedience, but who pushed the boundaries of the ancient monastic system so that their work in the world was combined with a more personal than communal prayer life. By the death of Ignatius, there were about three thousand Jesuits scattered all over Europe and much of the known world. The network of Jesuit schools, mostly for the upper echelons of European society, spread the Tridentine spirit of reform to all areas, even before the Council itself had happened. Teresa of Avila had longed for a few decent priests. Here they were in abundance. The Jesuits were a wholly male and hierarchical institution and were deliberately intent on ignoring women, except, interestingly enough, fallen women. Since Pope Gregory I had redesigned the apostle Mary Magdalene into a fallen woman, there was a certain attraction built into the redemption of such women to lives of repentance. The Jesuits provided a local and very effective infrastructure to the work of reform, at least for men. This is not surprising, since the reigning pope, Paul IV, is known as one of the most absolute misogynists who ever occupied the chair of Peter.

The early years of Teresa of Avila were spent in relative distraction and aimlessness, but a major conversion experience occurred around the age of forty in 1554. Teresa acknowledged that she had received some very bad spiritual direction from priests who did not know what they were doing, and she began to design her own map of the spiritual life. Her initial aim was to reform Carmel and return to what was called the primitive observance. This new group was called the Discalced Carmelites. Teresa met huge resistance at every hand's turn, both inside and outside Carmel. She was always under the eye of the Spanish Inquisition and after the publication of the Index of Forbidden Books by Paul IV in 1559, she had to clear her bookshelves of several volumes. Her goals for reform merged with the Tridentine goals of conformity of belief and uniformity of worship, even though Teresa seemed, in many ways, to be unaware of Trent, and certainly unaware of the Protestant Reform. What Teresa provided, however, was a map of the inner spiritual journey which was provided initially for women, but spread like wildfire throughout Europe. Eventually Teresa was instructed to write down her teachings and, reluctantly at first, she began to write. It is impossible to look at her whole corpus of writings, including about four hundred letters and several books, but one of her last writings, *The Interior Castle,* has come to be recognised as a great Catholic mystical classic. Her writings were in an informal and conversational style and they spread all over the world, and initiated a reform of the inner life of prayer among people of all classes, which had been missing from the Christian scene for centuries.

In 1567 Teresa met John of the Cross, who was twenty-five while she was in her fifties. Together they set out to reform both female and male sections of the Carmelite world, and Teresa said her aim was to found as many convents as there were hairs on her head.

Teresa hated false devotion and the kinds of fanciful mysticism that were occasionally to be found, even in her own convents. She set out to provide a basis for a true spiritual life based on an intense awareness of God's presence and a deep love for the humanity of Jesus. It is remarkable that so many women mystics discover their humanity and root their spiritual life in the humanity of Jesus. Even the use of the name of Jesus is almost peculiar to women, even though Vincent de Paul later acknowledged that his spiritual life had changed only when he started using this name. Teresa experienced many visions and interactions with the divine, whom, in the context of the growing Spanish empire, it is not surprising that she called 'His Majesty'. Like the medieval women mystics Teresa believed that this spiritual journey was open to all. It was based on friendship with God and always led to outward ministry. Again, like so many other mystics, Teresa ceased to look externally for God, but found God at the centre of her own life.

The most brilliant, and perhaps most well known of Teresa's works, as we have said, is *The Interior Castle*. Here she traces seven dwelling places where the spiritual traveller rests on the way to God. The foundation of the whole journey is self-knowledge, which, like Catherine of Siena and other women mystics, is the door to the mystery of God's presence. The first three dwellings are for beginners and consist of clearing the decks for action, so to speak. The ancient initial task of purgation figured largely here, although Teresa was extremely practical in her attitude towards self-denial and mortification. She always emphasised proper eating and sleeping habits and did not want any penitential prima donnas in her communities.

The fourth dwelling is the turning point in the spiritual journey, and to put it simply, was a move from meditation to contemplation, from being self-directed to being wholly God-directed. Once Teresa enters this realm, as was true for other women mystics, her language becomes more poetic and metaphorical. Love is central to union and the language of Teresa is, in a sense, quite traditional in women's mystical writing, although she may not have been aware of the earlier women. She loves the idea of water flowing, transparent, cleansing. She speaks of moving from the reception of water via an aqueduct made with great skill by human hands and the springing up of water from the secret depths of the earth as an image of the move from meditation to contemplation. Another striking image of one's interaction with God is the falling of rain drops on a river or the arrival of a stream at the ocean, where the union of stream and sea is invisible but real. This image, though there is no evidence that Teresa could have been aware of it, was also used, as we have seen, by Marguerite Porete as she described the Seine entering the sea, and then not knowing where the river ends and the sea begins. One of the best-known metaphors of Teresa is the silkworm which eventually produces a 'little white butterfly', an image for Teresa of the soul's ascent to God.

Teresa also uses the image of marriage with its rhythm of meeting, getting to know each other, betrothal and union, as an image of the spiritual journey that would be available to all. She was intent on calling all to make this journey, and as we shall see, her call to spiritual growth was heard by thousands. Wherever a Carmelite convent arrived, the writings of Teresa followed and many women embraced the teaching of Teresa. Since love was central to her teaching and, as Teresa taught, love must never be idle, the spiritual journey began to produce the works of education and healing which have characterised the life of women religious for hundreds of years. Her practical wisdom taught people that if they were in doubt about their ability to love God, they need never be in doubt about the love of one's neighbour, real and present to all. No one needed permission to make this journey, Teresa taught, an instruction which is light years from the strict and rigid spiritual life advocated by the Council of Trent and based on the Catechism and sound doctrine. As the Tridentine tradition was closing down Catholic intellectual life in actions such as producing the Index of Forbidden Books, Teresa was inviting people, all people, to stretch themselves to the very limits of their humanity, where, with the humanity of Jesus, they would meet and feel co-natural with God.

At no time in the sixteenth century, or in any other century, were women fully integrated into the ecclesial life of Catholicism. As the Tridentine Catholic Church began to take its post-Reformation shape, the male clerical nature of church life became more and more apparent. Priests held the keys to the grace of God in the sacrament of Penance. They controlled where and when people could approach the Eucharist. After Trent, the clergy had more and more control over marriage. Fear of God came to be central to the public life of the Church with greater emphasis on sin, original sin, the devil, hell and purgatory. People were almost terrorised into believing and as the sacrificial nature of the Eucharist became more and more pronounced, people felt more and more unworthy of participating. One consolation for the ordinary person was the new emphasis on devotion to Mary through the Rosary. Since the defeat of the Turks at the Battle of Lepanto in 1570, and the attribution of this victory to Mary through the Rosary, by Pope Pius V, this devotion to Mary began again to grow in popularity. Where the Tridentine God seemed harsh and unrelenting, Mary was accessible and comforting. As we shall see in the next chapter, devotion to Mary, particularly as it was neglected by the Protestants, became a major feature of Tridentine Catholic life.

One of the major centres where Teresa's writings and her convents began to have huge influence on the life of the Church, particularly on the lives of women, was France. As we have seen, the Council of Trent acted as if totally unaware of the presence of women in the Church. They were not really considered to be part of ecclesial life at all. They were silent, invisible, and expected to contribute nothing. In fact through the actions of Eve, women were seen as a kind of negative equity in the Church, dragging it down and being especially destructive to the newly-exalted celibate clergy. So no pope or council or member of the clergy higher or lower set about the task of calling women to serve the Church in the ministries of education and healing. This was entirely the work of women alone. It is historically demonstrable that as the male clerical Church closes down its range of interest, the women of the Church emerge in huge numbers to take their place as the baptised Christians that in fact they are. This is precisely what happened after Trent. Within a few decades, hundreds of women's orders had emerged and groups of women were founding hospitals, orphanages, schools and refuges for the homeless. They were even travelling to the far corners of the globe as missionaries, another area completely ignored by the Council. For the next several hundred years it was these women who worked to influence the lives of thousands of believers, and without them, despite the fact that the women were ignored, the work of the Church could not have been carried out. The rise of hundreds of religious orders was against a backdrop of a revived fear and distrust of women, and in some places outright misogyny. The horrific witch-burnings, which continued after the Reformation, only spread this fear and women became the scapegoats of a society filled with dread. The utterly appalling *Malleus Maleficarum* had been published in 1484, advising inquisitors on how to spot, torture and execute witches. It was written by two Dominicans at the request of the pope, and thereby gained authoritative standing. It left a niggling horror of women in the Church for centuries. It recalled all the old 'arguments' against women from the Letter to Timothy, through Augustine, Aquinas and added its own lunatic assessment of women. They were created second, sinned first, were daughters of Eve, spawn of the devil, had to be kept under obedience, and added that many women were having sex with the devil and therefore castrating men. It was a total call to arms against women. Above all, women could not speak or teach or be seen to act publicly on behalf of the Church.

By the seventeenth century, this dread of women and their carnality had become a literary quarrel, as we have seen, and the arguments for and against the dangers of women, and for and against their ability to think like human beings, was being argued at every level. It was clearly a man's world and a man's Church. Real virtue was male virtue and women in religious life followed, as always, rules that had been written by men for men.

But the walls of the French Church – the Gallican Church – were about to be breached. Carmelite convents began to open in France, bringing with them the writings of Teresa of Avila. French women turned to this new spiritual invitation with alacrity and enthusiasm. This was aided by the invention of the printing press which now began to make the writings of Teresa of Avila available in the vernacular. We will be concentrating on France here, for convenience, but similar movements were taking place in England with the courageous genius of Mary Ward (1585–1645) and in Italy with the originality and spiritual wisdom of Angela Merici (1474–1544). The works of Teresa gave rise to a profound religious revival which spread rapidly through-out France and all of Europe. There were by now over fifty Carmelite convents in France and these were the epicentre of this revival. Women gathered in groups to make Teresa's instruction on active love a reality and by the mid-seventeenth century there were more of these religious – *les devotes* – than there were priests and monks in France. All of these groups were begun at the initiative of women, under the leadership of women and organised with the intelligence and faithful devotion of women.

The words 'intrusion' and even 'invasion' were beginning to be heard again. Women were invading the Church of God and its ministry. While initially the Church did everything in its power to resist them, eventually the local bishops realised that they could not survive without them and they set about taking over the leadership and organisation of these women. It is here that the phrase 'covering their disobedience with a cloak of obedience' really comes into focus. Later generations of these great women founders, having been brow-beaten and indoctrinated by the Tridentine reform, spoke of their women founders as obedient women dedicated to the carrying out of the popes' and bishops' wishes. All the women sounded alike, as their distinct personalities were submerged beneath a surface veneer of required Catholic womanly virtue. The women became paragons of Tridentine perfection, as each became a model of the required virtues rather than a distinct woman genius.

More recently, as the sources for the real lives of these women emerge, it is possible and delightful to discover that they were not all cut from the same Tridentine cloth, but powerful strong-minded women who knew exactly how to run rings around their supposed spiritual directors and Episcopal superiors, even as they professed verbal obedience. If this had not happened, it is now clear that none of the women's communities would have survived the male imposition of supposed womanly virtue. But the women's work of education, healing, running orphanages and housing the homeless was so brilliantly done that eventually the Church and society had to accept them.

The presence of these women raised all kinds of theological and ecclesiological problems for the male-dominated Church. If these women were going to work in public and resist cloister, then they could not be called nuns. Both society and the church were caught between prejudice and appreciation. It is like a return to the questions raised by the Beguines of the Middle Ages. Who are these women? Who sent them? Who are they obeying? What rule are they following? The spontaneous devotion and enthusiasm of the women was gradually housed in a quasi-cloistered state, and rules were imposed on them, but the church could not halt the work or penetrate the environs of the convents.

Not all of these convents were successful, of course, nor all of the nuns as devoted as they might have been. But the vast majority were faithful to their commitments and left their stamp of devotion on generations of Catholic women and men.

One of the gifts of this new form of religious community life was that it gave women a choice between marriage and the convent. Within marriage, patriarchal marriage, women were without choice or initiative. Within the convent structure, women ran schools, hospitals, handled huge sums of money, made decisions for hundreds of people, directed the construction of huge institutions and were trained as teachers, nurses and social workers. Protestant women, confined to the structure of patriarchal marriage had no such choices or opportunities. The one new role for the Protestant woman was that of parson's wife, a role that was as confining as it may have been prestigious at the local level.

Two brief examples of this movement will now be examined in the persons of Jane de Chantal and Louise de Marillac, with their friends, companions and co-workers, Francis de Sales and Vincent de Paul respectively. It is part of the context of this new movement that these two couples saw each other, not as superior and inferior, but as equals.

Jane de Chantal (1567–1641) was a woman of enormous spiritual depth and gifts of intellect and pastoral sensitivity. Jane and her brother were raised by their father, their mother having died at the birth of her son. They received a thorough education with emphasis on the practical subjects of finance and law, and these were to serve Jane very well in later life as director of community. At the age of twenty-eight, Jane's husband died suddenly in a freak accident and she was left to raise her surviving four children. Nine years later, her intense grief had changed into an intense thirst for God and a hunger for a deep spiritual life, Jane met Francis de Sales, who in 1602 had become Bishop of Geneva, with a desire to re-convert the old city of Calvin. Francis de Sales had struggles in his early life about the sufferings of Jesus and the condemnation of humans by God for this suffering. With the help of a Jesuit spiritual director, he came to realise that love is God's design and purpose, and, whatever about the next life, we can always love God here and now, wherever we are, and that everyone can do this. A strain of quiet optimism runs through the whole of the spirituality of Francis de Sales, and this was bolstered by the practice of mutual friendship, when he met Jane de Chantal.

This notion of female/male mutuality was entirely new in the Christian tradition, and indeed in the secular tradition. Women were considered to be incapable of such mutuality and were designed by God, for auxiliary rather than equal roles. Even today, this notion of mutuality is still a desideratum rather than an actual experience, especially since the Catholic Church has moved from the explicit expression of women's inferiority to a prescribed and unchanging underling role.

The mutual friendship of Jane and Francis was based on an intimate knowledge of and relationship with the human Jesus. This mutual friendship of the two was intended to spread outward to all. To illustrate this basic spiritual relationship both Jane and Francis inscribed the words 'Live Jesus' on all their correspondence. They both declared that they had given birth to each other and their intuitive Jesus-centred relationship governed all their interactions.

The seventeenth century dawned on a new age. Religious wars were waging, modern vernaculars were emerging, Copernicus and Galileo were reshaping the mental geography of the human mind and the Tridentine reform was at last beginning to make some headway in the Catholic Church. New exegesis of Scripture was underway as well as new forms of philosophy and theology, even though the rigidity of the Council of Trent kept all this within the bounds of the Catholic Church, it could no longer control what was happening in the new Protestant communities.

In the midst of all this the vocation to love, adopted by both Jane and Francis calls to mind the teaching of Julian of Norwich, which was probably quite unknown to them, that God loves all and wills the salvation of all. It is at this time that, in a sense, the outer and inner forms of Christian life begin to diverge. Outwardly, the Church takes on the appearance of a harsh, unbending institution with rigid rules reaching into the most intimate cores of human life. Inwardly, a new awareness of God's love, promulgated by many new religious communities and the occasional bishop like Francis de Sales, begins to develop into the modern, usually false, distinctions between religion and spirituality.

By 1610, Jane and Francis had co-founded the Visitation community who would spread this practical love of God at all levels of society. During their lifetime, eighty convents were founded in France.

The community of the Visitation was founded for people like Jane who were desirous of a more intense spiritual life but who, because of family commitments, could not, or did not wish to, join one of the old established and cloistered religious communities. They wanted a religious community where there would be much 'coming and going', as a later critic described these communities. The women could become 'daughters of prayer' in the context of a much simplified monastic routine, and continue to exercise their work of visiting the poor and the sick.

Jane lived in this community as others were expected to live. She had care of the properties of both her father and father-in-law, and was involved in the lives of her children and their marriages. But all did not go according to plan. The second convent of the Visitation was founded at Lyons and the Archbishop was a strong Tridentine follower. He simply would not accept women who lived like this without any apparent precedent that he was aware of. There was a lengthy correspondence and much debate between the two bishops, but eventually the Tridentine reformer won and the women of the Visitation were cloistered against their will. Since there was no way the Archbishop was going to have a theological discussion with a woman, even a revered woman, as Jane now was, it was left to her colleague to argue the case. Francis, who was engaged in the writing of his own *magnum opus* on the spiritual life, *Treatise on the Love of God*, tried to educate the Archbishop of Lyons on the position of women, but failed utterly. He wrote:

> Woman ... no less than man, enjoys the favour of having been made in the image of God; the honour is done equally to both the sexes; their virtues are equal; to each of them is offered an equal reward, and, if they sin, a similar damnation. I would not want woman to say, I am frail, my condition is weak. This weakness is of the flesh, but virtue, which is strong and powerful, is seated in the soul.

In actual fact, the parents of the Visitation sisters and the people of Lyons in general, supported their Archbishop. They could not envisage how this new community would work in practice. Parents wanted their daughters to stay cloistered in their convents. They did not want them returning home to upset family arrangements. And so, one of the most visionary and pro-woman innovations of the seventeenth-century Church, was stopped almost before it started.

The spirituality of the Salesians and the nuns of the Visitation continued, even though it was in muted form. When rediscovered in its original form in recent years, its radical nature is apparent. France and Europe generally in the seventeenth century was not ready for any change whatsoever on the position of women. It was not only a spiritual and theological argument, but one that reached into the heart of politics and of society. Whatever changes were taking place in society, the position of women was not going to change. It continued to be a male-dominated church and in society, and male-led households and convents were seen as the only norm. The teaching voice of women was again suppressed, and the innovative nature of the writings and conversations of Jane and Francis was forgotten.

Nowadays, commentators draw out several dimensions of this spirituality of Jane and Francis, which are deeply relevant in today's Church and world. It is rooted in Christian humanism, which emphasises the innate dignity of every human person. Human nature has been wounded by sin but it is not corrupt and each human has a deep natural orientation towards the God of love and compassion. We are called to live between the 'two wills of God', that is the will of God manifest in the events over which we have no control, and the will of God manifest in our own lives as we journey on the spiritual path. God is available to all and can be found in the midst of everyday life. There is no need to head for the desert or into a cloistered convent. At our creation, we were gifted with a spacious liberty which leaves us free to choose. We do not need methods and plans for this. One is reminded of the teaching of Marguerite Porete, that we must learn to 'live without a why'. We can always live in God's presence. Our spiritual life arises from the inner spring of the heart. We need direction and sometimes discernment, but we do not need to add any further mortification to the natural trials of our everyday lives. And foreseeing the teaching of St Thérèse of Lisieux, we are invited to do all the little things with the greatest of love.

Such spiritual guidance sounds so modern and seems to be entirely at cross purposes with the Tridentine reform and its emphasis on rigidity and doctrinal orthodoxy, rooted as it is in a total distrust of the human person. Indeed a huge and extremely destructive argument waged theologically across Europe on the notion of personal freedom. Religious orders and dioceses took sides. Bishops raged against bishops. And, in the end, the Jansenist rigorist stream prevailed over the Salesian freedom, even though Janseism in its essence was condemned. At the same time, as a result of the feuding of Bishops Bossuet and Fenelon on these issues, an event that has been named the 'rout of the mystics' occurred. This was a denunciation of the kind of prayer of the presence of God that both Jane and Francis and many others now practiced, and that went back to the women of the Middle Ages. It left the Church for centuries in the thrall of a heartless and disembodied kind of orthodox spirituality that starved many people of any real contact with God. This will be of later interest to us. For now, we can turn to another couple of seventeenth-century friends who were contemporaries and friends of Jane de Chantal and Francis de Sales, namely Louise de Marillac (1591–1660) and Vincent de Paul (1581–1660).

The first of the Bourbon kings, Henry IV, had on 25 July 1593, knelt on the steps of Notre Dame and renounced Protestantism, with his much quoted remark that 'Paris was worth a Mass'. His subsequent behaviour was not much influenced by this act since he was mostly allied with the Protestant states against Spain. His dream of royal absolutism was finally realised in his grandson Louis XIV (1647–1715), but the political and religious society of France was moving in the same direction as the Catholic Church, that is, totally centralised power. The Council of Trent had been promulgated in 1564, but it had never been received in France. The early life of Vincent de Paul gives us a sense of how weak and disjointed the Gallican Church was. Vincent became a priest for the sole purpose of improving the living conditions of his family, which was part of the normal clerical career path. He hoped to acquire a few benefices that would enrich him and his family, as Pope Paul III and almost every cleric had done. The growing spiritual vitality in several parts of France, as a result of the Carmelite and Jesuit reform movements, seems initially not to have touched Vincent at all.

After a meeting with Francis de Sales and Jane de Chantal in 1621, and after several encounters with the poor, ignorant Catholics on the estate where he was chaplain, Vincent discovered his true vocation, namely to care for the poor, who henceforth were his 'master'. Vincent called on other priests to join him and began to organise missions to the poor and neglected and to care for their pastoral and physical needs. In 1624, he first met Louise de Marillac, an aristocratic young widow with a son, who was spiritually insecure, but like Jane de Chantal, had brilliant gifts of administration and organisation. In a reversal of the usual stereotypes of female/male relationships, she was obviously the head, he the heart, of all their future endeavours. They were friends for thirty-six years with the same kind of mutuality that had marked the friendship of Jane and Francis. Initially, Louise needed the guidance and encouragement of Vincent, but, after the founding of her community, the Daughters of Charity in 1633, Louise grew to accept her gifts and to use her power and organisational skills. Following Vincent's example, she turned her gaze away from her own life towards Jesus and the poor. Their spirituality was likewise motivated by the human life of Jesus and it is noteworthy that both began to use the name of Jesus as the central core of their spiritual life and prayer.

Their lives and communities were devoted to the service of the poor, and, as often happens, an avalanche of projects followed upon their initial steps. They not only cared for the poor and neglected in their own homes, but also visited prisons, the galleys, the wounded on the battlefield and so it went on. Wherever there was a need, there they were.

Louise organised one of the first hospices for those who were aged and poor and her creativity shines through in her ability to care for both body and spirit. She organised her hospice so that the aged could live in beautiful surroundings and even provided occupational therapy, something quite unheard of until then. Both Vincent and Louise always preferred a home-based ministry but their very successes caused them to have to institutionalise their work. This multifaceted ministry of Louise was rooted in a study of Scripture and in the annual round of liturgical celebration. Louise spoke of a mysticism of the group, where all the sisters would move forward together in love and support. We have over four hundred letters of instruction in spirituality from Louise to her sisters and they are a storehouse of practical and mystical teaching. As well as being an advocate for the poor, Vincent de Paul was a trained canon lawyer, and it was his skill in this area which preserved Louise from the trammels of cloister. The sisters took private vows and were instructed by Vincent on how to deal with bishops and their Tridentine concerns. The Daughters of Charity were utterly devoted to working with the poor, and if local bishops tried to interfere, the sisters just left the area. This tactic was very successful, at a time when the poor were seen generally as a threat to society, and not as victims or witnesses to God's love. Louise's sisters showed no outward sign of being religious in the traditional sense, but they lived, prayed, and acted as religious. This 'holy deviousness' is characteristic of many women's groups as they tried to follow their calling without the interference of rigidly orthodox clergy. The city streets were to be their cloister and the service of the poor was to take precedence over the ancient monastic office and routine. Louise called this way of acting 'leaving God for God'. Eventually, bishops in many parts of France were crying out for their services.

Both Vincent and Louise died in 1660. During the following years courageous French women like Marguerite Bourgeois and Marguerite d'Youville brought the Word of God to far-flung and newly-'discovered' mission territories, and these women can be recognised as the true founders of places like Montreal and Quebec in New France, or Canada. All these women took the initiative to follow the gospel precedent themselves. They were instructed by no pope or bishop, and even though the Council of Trent influenced huge swathes of Christian society in the following centuries, it was all these women who took upon themselves the task of ministry in ways totally inconceivable to the Tridentine bishops who led the Church through the following centuries. Their part has been brushed over in silence or attributed to male clerics, but it was women's initiative and ingenuity and complete devotion to the humanity of Jesus that changed the face of the Church for ordinary people.

The pattern of women's contribution to the life of the Christian Church is beginning to become clear. While men struggled with the problems of wealth and greed and made efforts to reform the church from the centre, women actually took their faith and the following of Jesus seriously, and without any call or clerical direction, they set out to follow the Gospel on their own initiative, and with their own spiritual integrity and ingenuity. These women mentioned here are just a few of the vast horde of women religious who brought the Gospel all over the world. Of course they were not alone, as many men also followed this path, but the men had the support, guidance and encouragement of the official Church, while the women had to struggle to establish their right as women to live and engage in ministry in this fashion. And one of the key elements in all the theology, spirituality and ministry of women throughout the ages, even from biblical days, was the following and imitation of Jesus.

The Marian Influence

One of the standard replies to any query about the position of women in the Catholic Church has always been: 'Look at the position of Mary, the Mother of God.' It is pointed out that she has been elevated above all others through the centuries, and that therefore women are more honored in the Church than anyone else, and should rejoice in their high estate in the person of Mary. There is usually an addendum about the unedifying spectacle of women seeking power, always of course, made by men who have not the slightest intention of relinquishing any of their power to women.

So what is the position of Mary? A recent book, *The Testament of Mary* by Colm Tóibín, attempts, in a fictional way, to place this question on Mary's lips, thus turning the whole question upside down. For whether fictionally or in reality, the position of Mary, as of all other women in Christianity, has been articulated by men. And as Tóibín's fictional Mary illustrates truthfully, Mary is told who she is and must be by men, rather than being asked to speak for herself. For even the greatest woman in the 'greatest story ever told' is silent and silenced.

Attitudes towards and teaching about Mary have changed significantly through the centuries. She has been used as a weapon against women, and against the Protestants, and as the guardian and saviour of the Church against warring infidels. She has also been claimed by the 'ordinary' people as their refuge, their comforter, their intercessor with a distant God. She has been elevated in doctrine and invoked in liturgy. She has formed a central part of the prayer and spiritual lives of millions through the ages, and she has been welcomed in vision and apparition at every stage of Christian history. In the Roman Catholic Church, Mary is everywhere, portrayed in brilliant and awe-inspiring art and again in cheap and shoddy plastic representations. This ubiquitous presence has been used by the people against the clergy and by the clergy against the people. As we can see from a historical overview of her symbolic presence in the Roman Catholic Church, she has accumulated images and metaphors that frequently clash and contradict each other, but have been woven into a mesmerising whole by centuries of the peoples' devotion.

There is no doubt that there was a real young Jewish woman who was the mother of Jesus. This historical figure, however, is by now, and has been almost from the beginning, way beyond our grasp. Mary, the historical woman, has played little part in the Marian story, except to give a factual basis to the human reality of Jesus. Even here, however, the historical details of her motherhood have been spiritualised into an unreal version of a non-human birth, surrounded by all kinds of supposedly grace-filled details, in order to separate this woman – from the very beginning – from all other women, and this birth from all other births. This development took place over centuries, right up to our own times. Once the historical details were removed, Mary became available for all kinds of symbolic expansions. The gospel of Luke may have begun this development by equating Mary with Hannah, the mother of Samuel, and by putting Hannah's words into Mary's mouth in the Magnificat.

For the first three hundred years, however, some historical elements of the Marian story remained in place, and since the Christian people were so intent on discovering the mystery of the human Jesus, the role of Mary was left practically untouched, and there seems to be little of what was later called Marian devotion. Christians of the first few hundred years recognised that Jesus had brothers and sisters, they knew the names of the brothers at least, and were content to let the motherhood of Mary stand as a reality. As would have been true for all young Jewish women, she was virginal until the birth of Jesus, an ordinary birth, despite the gospel additions of shepherds and kings. There was very little theological reflection on Mary except the statements from Irenaeus of Lyons in the second century, as the canon of the New Testament was being formulated, that Mary was the new Eve. This one theological dictum opened the door to the eventual portrayal of Mary as the precise mirror opposite of Eve, and therefore of all other women who had, since the Letter to Timothy, assumed the role of 'daughters of Eve'. These two images of women have been played upon down through the centuries with endless variations. Mary was obedient, Eve disobedient; Mary spoke to an angel, Eve to the Serpent/Devil; Mary said *Fiat*, let it be done unto me, Eve rejected God's command and tried to change the course of God's plan; Mary brought salvation, Eve brought destruction. In each case, the Eve side of the list of contrasts included all other women, daughters of Eve. The early Fathers of the Church had a field day with these images, and by the end of the third century, the symbolic gap between Mary and ordinary women had widened irreparably.

It was the actions of some of these ordinary women that radically changed the direction of Marian devotion. By the middle of the fourth century many women in the large cities of the Roman Empire, like Rome and Milan, had, in imitation of the mothers and fathers of the desert, opted for a life beyond and without marriage. This was an inconceivable idea in the ancient world. First of all, marriage and submission to a husband was the standard expectation of all women, whether pagan or Christian. But these new Christian women renounced marriage in their thousands. Secondly, it was widely believed, in a wonderful demonstration of male projection, that women were wholly carnal and responsible for all male sexual temptation, and totally incapable of virginity. When the Christian Church was faced with thousands of women who were doing precisely that, namely living lives of total virginity, the Church leaders went into a state of panic. When, moreover, women then insisted on exercising leadership in their own communities, the 'Fathers' were apoplectic. Male argumentation went on for decades between Church leaders like Jerome, Ambrose and Augustine on one side and Jovinian, Helvidius and Pelagius on the other. The Christian Church was beginning to accept the value of women's virginity as the ultimate solution to the problematic presence of women in the Church. Virginity seemed to solve all the women problems. As Augustine said, 'Let the pagans copulate', and then Christianity would turn the women into virgins. Problem solved. The doctrine of virginity for women and for men became central to the church's sense of itself. Virginity, and its companion obedience, became the church's main approach to women. Virginity was superior to all other virtues, and thus separated the Church into first-class and second-class Christians. The higher virginity was praised, the lower became the status of marriage as a kind of permanent sinful state organised around the practice of sexual intercourse and motherhood.

On the other side, which from the very beginning of the debate was a lost cause, were Jovinian and his colleagues, who argued that baptism was central to the Christian identity, and whether one was single, married, widowed or virginal, it made no difference in God's eyes, since baptism was the criterion for being a Christian. This side was painted as sexual enthusiasts, doubt was cast on their personal lives, marriage and pregnancy were ridiculed, and gluttony and every other conceivable evil was attributed to them. Eventually, the battle was totally lost when Mary was brought into the debate as the virgin of virgins.

This debate was taking place in the context of the fundamental Christian debate about the reality of Jesus and the interrelationship of his humanity and divinity. As the Council of Nicea, followed by the Councils of Constantinople and Ephesus, established as essential Christian doctrine the Trinitarian divinity of Jesus, the question of Mary's identity came to be of profound importance. Jesus, divine and human, could not possibly have come into the world as all other humans did. His mother must have been out of the ordinary. Augustine developed the notion of Mary's vow of virginity, Jerome demonstrated that the brothers and sisters of Jesus were actually cousins, and that therefore Mary was a perpetual virgin, and Ambrose ransacked the Hebrew bible for foretellings of Mary's role in the biblical phrases, Tower of Ivory, House of Gold, Ark of the Covenant and all the other invocations that eventually formed the Litany of Loreto.

There was no arguing with any of this. Those who supported baptismal inclusion and the dignity of marriage were silenced for centuries, and a huge outburst of Marian devotion took over the Christian Church. Mary was portrayed as Queen of Heaven, as 'unlike all other women as possible'. In a phrase that echoed down through the centuries, *potuit, decuit, fecit*, Mary accumulated all possible honours that differentiated her from all other women. The phrase implies that whatever honour was being considered for Mary was possible for God to accomplish (*potuit*). Furthermore it was fitting that God should do this (*decuit*). And therefore God accomplished this in Mary (*fecit*). Enormous enthusiasm greeted these developments and Mary's heavenly place was firmly rooted within Christianity for centuries. Churches were dedicated in her honour, hymns were written, and litanies composed. Whole sections of Scripture were reinterpreted to include these new teachings, and virgins took their place, willy-nilly, at the forefront of Christian life. The question of Christian marriage was postponed for centuries, and is still one of the most controversial and intractable issues in the Roman Catholic Church.

One of the most significant results of this outburst of theological activity concerning Mary, the Mother of Jesus, now also *theotokos,* God-bearer and Queen of Heaven and symbolically represented in a new exalted place in heaven, is that the people took her to themselves. It is interesting that the name 'Mother of God' was rarely used officially in the early Church, having too many reminiscences of the many pagan God-mothers of the time. We hear of the first torchlight processions in her honour in Ephesus after the Council there proclaimed her *theotokos* in 431. This love affair between Mary and the people has only developed through the centuries and each century has added its own particular colour to the devotion.

This popular dimension was increased enormously in the tenth century when a popular folktale became a mainstream teaching. It was called *The Legend of Theophilus* and related the story of how Mary countermanded God's order with regard to the eternal damnation of Theophilus and rescued him from hell. This later became the basis of the *Faust* story. Mary became the peoples' intercessor and intervener between the people and a justly angry God. She was invoked as the patron of a happy death and in a world preoccupied with death, this was a huge source of comfort.

This popular dimension became all-embracing, as Mary symbolically moved from heaven to earth. In the newly-clericalised world of the High Middle Ages, as the clergy more and more controlled the channels of sacramental grace, Mary was the one channel freely and generously available to all. As the psalms recited in Latin came to be almost exclusively the preserve of the clergy, the new devotion of the Rosary, with its one hundred and fifty Hail Mary's brought Mary closer to the people and gave them a new means of access to God's graces.

Indeed the Rosary became a fairly brilliant means of catechesis for the multitudes who were excluded from the study of theology or from any real access to understanding the mystery of Christ. Prayer, both liturgical and personal in Latin, to the Father through Christ came to be the preserve of the clergy, while prayer in the vernacular to Mary was the channel open to all. The *Hail Mary*, which up until then consisted only of the biblical greeting of the angel Gabriel to Mary, was now lengthened to include 'pray for us sinners, now and at the hour of our death'. The addition of the *Pater Noster* and *Gloria patri*, as well as the reflection on the biblical mysteries, together with the addition of the Creed, made the Rosary the perfect tool of catechesis for the multitudes. The Rosary contained all they needed to know. For the vast majority of the non-clerical Church, the focus of faith and devotion switched from Jesus to Mary, and the prayers of the faithful centred on Mary, even to the extent, as we know from our childhood, of old people saying the Rosary during Mass.

With the renewed emphasis on the Sacrifice of the Mass, there was an outburst of reflection on the sufferings of Jesus in the events surrounding the Crucifixion, and Mary the Sorrowing Mother, gave people a sense of hope in the midst of despair that was not matched by any other spiritual dimension for centuries. Mary still retained her heavenly place ahead of all the angels and saints, but she was given, so to speak, a more democratic persona, as she became part of the lives of the people. Alongside the ancient biblical invocations from the time of Ambrose in the fourth century, she became *Our Lady of the Wayside, Star of the Sea, Mother of Sorrows, Comforter of the Afflicted*, and hundreds of other new titles were added to her devotional arsenal. It is no surprise, then, that apparitions of Mary begin to be reported from all corners of the Christian world. This Mary, who is now invoked by all, is perceived to be ever close at hand and ready with a word of comfort, and even a word of warning to those who try to abuse her generosity.

Several new prayers become part of the Marian prayer-package at this time, including the *Hail Holy Queen*, and the *Memorare*, which, as well as invoking Mary's name in praise and petition, sketch out the lineaments of a growing theology of Mary. The 'poor banished children of Eve' can now call on the 'Mother of Mercy' for all their needs, including their ultimate salvation, as Mary comes to be seen as a Co-Redemptrix with Jesus.

It seems that every group in Christendom begins to add its own dimension to the Marian complex of devotions. Religious orders add scapulars, religious guilds add new titles, and the saints add their own more theological reflections. Indeed, it was saints such as Bernard of Clairvaux, with his intense love of and devotion to Mary, who added strength and a kind of integrity to the devotion of the people. Bernard saw Mary as the neck of the Mystical Body, through whom all Godward prayer and invocation had to pass. It was Bernard who portrayed God the Father as a somewhat cantankerous parent, who was better not approached directly by the ordinary people. For their own protection, it was better for them to go through Mary, *per Mariam ad Jesum*, as the now centuries old dictum has it.

In this way, the Christian Church became a Marian community for the vast majority of its members, and this was reinforced with an enormous outpouring of art and statuary. While much of this art is brilliant and profoundly moving, it also adds a new secular dimension to Marian devotion, as she is portrayed as the pinnacle of beauty in whatever culture the artist called home. This vast devotional enthusiasm had little influence on the lives of real women. The highly-symbolic development of Marian devotion stood in the place of any reflection on women or their place in this new clericalised Church. While Mary was everywhere, women became more and more invisible and silenced. 'Look at Mary' was the response to any query about the position of women. There was Mary placed above the saints and angels and archangels, so it was obvious what the Church thought of women. This highly-symbolic figure, with practically all traces of humanity and womanhood removed, with no obvious sexual characteristics, and no hint whatsoever of any female carnality, was exactly what the Church wished for women – a fictional and highly-symbolic image which never existed and never could exist. She was 'as unlike all other women as possible' as the fourth-century Fathers of the Church had emphasised, and all other women were as far removed from Mary as it was possible to be.

It is no accident that exaggerations, theological and otherwise, entered into this picture of Mary. A last cry to Mary before death took the place, for many, of a committed Christian life. Whole generations of people lived and died in a kind of anti-chamber to Christianity, as their devotion to Mary substituted for any kind of biblically-based Christian understanding. While adding comfort and consolation to the lives of millions, the Christian Church stumbled along with a barely recognisable sense of what the gospel message had demanded. It is no wonder then, that Reformation theology, as it developed, quickly disposed of all non-biblical elements of Marian devotion, and eventually Mary was moved to the periphery of the many developing Protestant Churches.

In response, the Council of Trent re-emphasised all aspects of 'traditional' Marian devotion, so that the Roman Catholic Church, as it emerged from the sixteenth-century confusion of faiths, took on a distinctly Marian air. In fact, devotion to Mary and adherence to the Marian doctrines soon became a test of Roman Catholic orthodoxy. The rosary was installed as the main form of prayer for the vast majority of Catholic members, and the festivals of Mary were celebrated with public enthusiasm, as a distinct rebuke to the unfaithful Protestants. Mary was never named a goddess. She was safe in her official position of *hyperdulia*, a kind of veneration above the saints and below the Trinity. But there is no doubt whatsoever that she was treated like a goddess and presumed to be able to act like one. She was the Queen reigning beside Christ the king. She was, in Bernard of Clairvaux's reckoning, quite capable of turning the divine plan upside down for her clients. Bernard called on the usual pattern of behaviour of the ordinary patriarchal family, where children learned that it was best to approach their father through their mother. Although Bernard's writings on Mary are only a very small part of his total output of brilliant theology, it was the brilliant reputation of Bernard who made the popular devotion to Mary central to Catholic identity, and gave it a cachet of official recognition.

In the Tridentine period, during the next several hundred years, there was no doubt whatsoever that Mary was the core devotion of Catholics. With a Latin liturgy that people were not even expected to understand, but attend faithfully, Mary offered a sense of comfort at every stage of human life. As the official language about Mary came to be more and more centred on her pure and sinless state, and the motherhood of Mary was elevated far above the motherhood of the ordinary woman, in the continued exploration of Mary's purity, as compared to all other women, the position of women and attitudes towards women diminished accordingly. With the proclamation of Mary's Immaculate Conception (1854), in the mid-nineteenth century, the stage was set for a new outpouring of love and devotion towards Mary. The nineteenth-century form of this devotion was the phenomenon of the Marian apparition, where Mary was seen to come personally to guide and warn and encourage members of the Catholic community in an age when multiple challenges to all forms of religion, especially perhaps Roman Catholicism, began to make their presence felt. From the time of the French Revolution, through the movement of thought called the 'Enlightenment', the old safe mostly aristocratic structures of society were crumbling. While efforts to reclaim all the *anciens regimes* of both church and state were attempted, the world took on a more democratic face, and the vast poverty and desperate situation of most of the world's populations were becoming apparent. Cries of outrage were coming from below rather than pompous pronouncements from above. While the Enlightenment accomplished a great deal in turning attention to what we now call human rights, it did nothing for the emotional and spiritual life of the vast majority of people. Within the Roman Catholic Church in general, it was always Mary who served this function best, and in a fairly worldwide demonstration of her concern, hundreds of Marian apparitions were reported. The scenarios were very similar. Mary was reported to appear to the very poor, mostly to children and usually in remote areas. This parallel source of revelation, so to speak, was a source of great anxiety to the official teaching body of the Catholic Church, as Mary left message after message to her soon to be millions of followers. Eventually the Church saw this phenomenon as a direct challenge to the Enlightenment with its heady mix of rational thought, historical critique and new biblical exegesis. The sites of Marian apparitions became magnets for millions and a whole new Marian industry grew up around these shrines, vastly aided, eventually, by the advent of air flight.

These Marian apparitions, in particular the 'approved' apparition sites of Lourdes and Fatima, and the more recent rather contentious site of Medjugorje, have left a very significant stamp on the devotional lives of millions. When one also recalls the earlier apparition of Mary at Guadalupe, and the widespread consequent devotion to her in Latin and South America, one can say that the whole Catholic world received a significant new Marian colouring.

The official Roman Catholic Church has always been cautious about this parallel *magisterium*. In a strictly hierarchical and patriarchal church, the advent of a movement from below is trying, to say the least. Even its 'approval' of pilgrimages and veneration of Mary at the apparition sites of Lourdes and Fatima is couched in cautious language. The actual event of the apparition is studied to remove all forms of adolescent illusion, psychological disturbance and perhaps diabolical influence. Then only a carefully worded permission to venerate Mary at this particular site is published. Even though many recent popes have expressed their own personal devotion to Mary in connection with these apparition sites, the official theological consensus is that all the theological conundrums raised by these events have to be carefully dealt with, especially for ecumenical reasons.

The use of the image of Mary as a kind of rearguard action against modernity has produced its own backlash in the Catholic Church. There is also present in this Marian devotion a kind of anti-clericalism, that has been evident in every generation. Mary belongs to the people, not to the clergy. Mary appears to them, not to the clergy. No pope, bishop, or priest has received a Marian apparition of this calibre. And so the conundrums continue.

As far as women are concerned, this devotion to Mary is precisely raised up as a countertone against all modern efforts to speak of the rights of women. This will be taken up later, but it is enough to point out here that devotion to Mary has delayed strenuously, rather than promoted, any efforts at promoting respect for the dignity and rights of women in the Catholic Church.

There is no doubt whatever that devotion to Mary has been a source of enormous consolation to millions of Catholic women worldwide. Mary has been present with them at birth and death and a source of encouragement in poverty, hardship and suffering. For most of these people, the theological difficulties of this symbolic elevation of Mary, has not been a source of concern. Mary, the Mother of all has Godlike powers of comfort and help. The theological questions about her quasi-humanity, and the questions this may raise about the humanity of her Son do not cause them any disquiet. But on the magisterial and theological front, these questions haunt those concerned with doctrinal orthodoxy. Are Jesus and Mary fully human or do they occupy some middle ground? Does Mary have quasi-divine powers or what precisely is her role in the Catholic firmament? When, in the mid-twentieth century, the Second Vatican Council was called, these questions preoccupied at least some of the participants. Some bishops saw the Council as an opportunity to proclaim more Marian titles and establish more Marian feast days. They wanted to continue to coast along with their people on this wave of Marian enthusiasm, which never seemed to wane. Other bishops, with a broader perspective, wished to examine several facets of Catholic doctrine, liturgy and scripture, and in this renewed perspective, to discover where Mary might most appropriately fit. These Marian minimalists and maximalists both saw their agendas turned upside down by the events of the Council, but in the end, it was the minimalists who won. The question of Mary was confined to Chapter Eight of the main document on ecclesiology, *Lumen Gentium*. For a Catholic world waiting for a new Marian revival, this was a kind of treason. There are many versions abroad today, fifty years after the Second Vatican Council, on the influence of the Council and its reception. But one certain perception at the time was that Mary had been demoted. New hints of anti-clericalism arose and a kind of underground reclamation of Mary was evident in many quarters. It was not until the next decade, in 1974, that Pope Paul VI, dealt officially with the question of Mary in his brilliant document, *Marialis Cultus*. Here he tries to establish a kind of contemporary persona for Mary as a strong, independent woman. He traces several bases for a correct form of Marian devotion, citing especially the necessity of a biblical foundation, a correct anthropological dimension and an ecumenical sensitivity. He further points to several liturgical reforms where the role of Mary is clearly made secondary to and auxiliary to that of her Son. Whatever welcome theologians may have given to this encyclical, it made very little impression on the Catholic populace, mostly as a result of bad or non-existent catechesis. The obvious Marian devotion of Pope John Paul II brought about an upsurge of Marian enthusiasm and even though Mary may not be as central to the lives of believers as formerly, her devotion and her pilgrimages are flourishing.

Wherever this traditional form of Marian devotion flourishes, the position of women languishes in a state of complete indifference. The Roman Catholic anomalies with regard to women continue in these circumstances. Women are present in the Church in great numbers. At any gathering of believers, except for clerical gatherings, women are in the majority. At the same time, nothing is expected of women. They have no official theological contribution to make. The Catholic Church does not need anything that women may want to say. Even still, in the Roman Catholic Church there is not one single theological reflection by a woman on the experience of conceiving, carrying, bearing or nourishing a child. No male theologian can do this. The one example of giving birth that has been appropriated by the Roman Catholic Church is the doctrinally taught, miraculous, virginal birth of Jesus by Mary, who was herself, as is also doctrinally taught, miraculously and immaculately conceived. Thus all female carnality has been removed from Church doctrine. Women's lives can never be a source for the doing of theology. The only life available for this is the life of the virgin mother, who can never be a model for the ordinary woman, who experiences intercourse, sexual orgasm, pregnancy, birthing, and breast-feeding. None of this is a resource for theology, even though Pope Francis welcomes breast-feeding women to his allocutions. As we saw, the medieval women mystics were very much aware of this and found the need to address their God as Mother. But even the elevation of four women to the status of Doctor of the Church, all of them virginal and long-dead nuns, has not altered this situation.

So the life experience of the vast majority of members of the church has been wiped out completely as a source for theology. Women's lives are irrelevant to the Church, even in the most central and essential core of their human being. Until this situation changes, the question of the ordination of women is a really secondary question. To what would women be ordained? To a priesthood that does not even recognise their full humanity? The mandatory celibacy of the Roman Catholic clergy is a continuous testimony to this deep-seated fear of women's bodies. And of course no taint of women's bodily and sexually active existence as wives, mothers and lovers is allowed to penetrate the wholly male mirroring of the Christian God. A long road has to be travelled by Roman Catholic women before any kind of official recognition of their presence, voice and undoubtedly essential ministry can take place. These questions will occupy us in the concluding chapters.

The Sixties:
Vatican II and Feminism

In the mid-sixties, for the first time since the 'intrusion' of the medieval women mystics into the Church, theology was being done in Christianity based on the experience of women, though not, of course, at the official level of the magisterium. This was a completely revolutionary event, since all of mainstream theology, all official Roman Catholic theology, has been done, and continues to be done, based only on the experience of men. When Pope Francis suggests a 'new' theology of women, he is speaking, one presumes, of men doing this, in other words, men telling women who they are in God's eyes and the eyes of the Church, what they should be doing and how they should be living their lives. The voices of women cannot contribute to this theology, nor are they expected to. The fact that there are now four women Doctors of the Church will not affect this situation.

So when Christian feminists began to speak of God and the things of God from the perspective and experience of women, this was a truly revolutionary event. The fact that it occurred in tandem with the calling of the Second Vatican Council added a particularly exhilarating dimension to the phenomenon. However, these two events were entirely unrelated. It would not have been conceivable to the bishop-participants of the Second Vatican Council that women could and did do a wholly different kind of theology. Absolutely nothing could have been further from their minds. And the women, using their own experience as a source for the doing of their theology, were not at all thinking in episcopal or male ecclesial terms. In fact they were doing precisely the opposite. They were exploring the things of God based on the experience of women and finding very different perspectives on God, on Scripture and on Church History. They were recasting male-inspired doctrines in female form and entering into the standard Christian male teachings on Redemption, Original Sin, Grace, Divinity, Trinity and Humanity from an entirely different direction. Even though the Roman Catholic Church has never admitted this, it is an entirely legitimate task the women set themselves. These women are baptised members of the Church with memories, brains, experiences and spiritual longings on which they can and do reflect. The fact that the Church has never desired to know about this reflection, or even considered it possible, is an enormous loss for the Church. It is losing the reflection of more than half its members. As the Church now struggles with 'falling numbers' and whole gener-ations of alienated women and men, it might be well to begin to notice that half the membership is female and that their theology is legitimate, and furthermore, is part of a continuous legitimate tradition from the very foundations of Christianity. So how did women fare theologically, in the mid-twentieth century?

Before looking at the Christian feminist agenda, it is important to look at the Second Vatican Council, because, despite the bishops' almost complete lack of concern for women, the Council had enormous consequences for them. Even though most ecclesiastical writing and teaching is supposedly generic, even though written in wholly male terms, the women of the Church universally read the Council in their own way. It is impossible to know if any bishop considered what it is like to be a woman and find oneself constantly addressed as if one were a man, but women, despite not being addressed directly, or even intentionally, heard the message of the Council. This was particularly so in five distinct areas running right through the Council documents, namely, Scripture, Ecclesiology, Liturgy, Ministry, and Spirituality. As an apparently wholly unintended consequence, women grasped the teaching of the Council in these areas and took it to themselves. The social context within which the Council took place, of course, had something to do with this, but there was a broader and longer tradition at work. From the very beginning of the Gospel story, women took the initiative. In the male-authored Gospel texts, there is no mention of women ever being called, as men were. We will never know whether or not this was the reality of the situation. But there is abundant evidence that, from the Gospel period on, women took the initiative to follow wherever there was the slightest opportunity. As we have seen, women disciples followed Jesus and without their witness, we would not even know the foundational stories. Throughout Christianity, wherever there was the merest suggestion of an open door, women 'intruded' on male Church affairs. Similarly, post-Vatican II, women 'received' the teaching of the Council in their own way, and thus changed the Church forever. It is because of this that all the post-conciliar popes have had to grapple with the question of women, because women 'intruded' on their consciousness in an entirely new way.

It was the women religious who led the way in the academic study of Scripture and in then proceeding to share their new insights with 'ordinary' women in parishes. It is not entirely accidental that theological colleges and institutes began opening their doors to women, even if one of the motivations was to boost the finances as the numbers of clerical students began to diminish. Initially, there were dozens of sympathetic male-authored books and articles on the roles of women in Scripture, and eventually the women began to write their own versions of these roles. After the publication of *Dei verbum*, the Dogmatic Constitution on Revelation, approaches to the interpretation of Scripture changed dramatically from the old literal or allegorical forms of interpretation to a more analytical and critical hermeneutic.

The Council had invited people to see the Gospels in a three-stage process: the text in hand, written several generations after the death of Jesus; the intervening oral tradition, when the stories were chosen and formed; and the actual historical events in the life of Jesus. With these tools of exegesis and hermeneutics, women then appeared as apostles, disciples, the only witnesses of the foundational events and the first preachers of the presence of the risen Jesus. As the openness of the attitude of Jesus towards women emerged, women were inspired and reawakened to their essential place in the living out of the Christian revelation. Women's self-perception changed dramatically. Initially, some of the energies of this new perception were sidetracked into a demand for the ordination of women. Along with the Church's definitively negative position on women's priestly ordination, came new official attempts to deal with women in a constructive way. If they were not the silent, submissive, homebound and husband-obeying creatures, then who were they? This question 'who are these women?' has traumatised the Church down through the centuries, and the official teachers have come up with increasingly less believable answers. Nevertheless, the Gospel tradition stands as testimony to the position of women in the life, words and acts of Jesus, and with each new proclamation of a 'New Evangelisation', women become more convinced of their position, and the Church more and more hesitant. It is a very dangerous memory.

The two documents on the Church *Lumen Gentium* and *Gaudium et Spes*, changed forever the nature of ecclesiology. The naming of the church as the People of God changed irrevocably the old structural divide between clergy and laity, at least in peoples' consciousness. The actual clerical structures have not really changed, except that many believers and also many clerics have consciously changed their attitudes and behaviour. The Catholic Church still insists on its essential hierarchical structure, but it is becoming harder and harder to insist on this in a world where equality at every level, disputes the sense of entitlement that hierarchy, especially patriarchal hierarchy, produces. Even the word 'laity' has its own problems of meaning, nevertheless the laity began to recognise the 'signs of the times' and make their own spiritual and moral decisions. As church architecture began to recognise the new ecclesiology in moving from the old hierarchical basilica style of church, to the more inclusive semi-circular design, peoples' perceptions changed almost imperceptibly. Obviously not everyone is happy about this, but the People of God have begun to claim their space and each new pope seems to be more aware of this.

In retrospect, as far as the People of God are concerned, perhaps one of the most important documents of the Council was *Perfectae Caritatis*, on the renewal of religious life. Women and men in religious orders were invited to return to the charism of their founders, and when they did so, they discovered women and men who were rather more revolutionary than they had been led to believe. Religious life was changed for ever, partly because of a huge exodus of women and men, partly because there were far fewer entrants, but especially because the self-perception of religious was completely changed. They no longer saw themselves as superior beings, perched somewhere between clergy and laity, but began to share their homes, their spirituality and their resources with the wider community. This was, perhaps, especially beneficial for women, who now had access to retreats, spiritual direction, spiritual traditions and education that they had been completely unaware of.

One of the remarkable outcomes of this democratisation of religious life was the sharing of what was initially called 'para-liturgy', a form of communal prayer, with word, symbol, song and silence, organised around a particular festival (like the Feast of Brigid of Ireland) or a particular season (like the winter or summer Solstice). In this way, the spiritual life of thousands of women was awakened, and they brought this new sense of God's presence to the celebration of the public worship of the Church.

The Eucharistic Liturgy itself was also changed almost beyond recognition by the Council, and there have been unceasing efforts to reclaim it and restore it to its former Tridentine glory days. When *Sacrosanctum Concilium* was published as the first major document of the Council, there was both delight and confusion. The introduction of vernacular languages was immensely important, as it had been ever since the translation of Scripture into the vernacular in the Middle Ages. Another democratisation of Christian life was taking place. New configurations of Church sanctuaries followed, along with congre-gational singing and vocal participation. Instead of being passive onlookers, people became participants, and began to evaluate the liturgy, often according to the behaviour of the celebrant, especially as homilist. The days of rosary recitation during Mass now disappeared, as the people had a very specific part to play in the celebration. Sacramental and other changes followed and, if truth be told, were implemented in a very uneven fashion. As the language of all the documents was invariably wholly male, addressed exclusively to men and brothers, women participants began to notice their total linguistic exclusion. Even with the odd addition of 'sisters' in some places, this still remains the case, and the linguistic exclusion has even been intensified since the renewed translation of the liturgy in recent times. As women attempt to participate in the Eucharist, they are invited to affirm that salvation is 'for us men and for our salvation'.

Women now have options. If they feel excluded, linguistically or otherwise, from the official public worship of the Church, there are other sources of worship in which they can participate. Again, this is almost exclusively provided by religious sisters as they invite people to share with them in renewing and celebrating their faith lives. It is obvious that for very many people the Sunday obligation is regarded with much less respect than formerly, and for thousands of younger women, the official liturgy offers no foothold whatever.

Throughout many of its documents, the Second Vatican Council tackled the subject of Ministry – papal, episcopal, priestly, diaconal and lay. It is astonishing to see history repeat itself so significantly in the explosion of lay interest in this new definition of ministry, from sacral cult to service of the community. As soon as the slightest opening is provided, women come rushing through and take the Church completely by surprise. The result is that the official Church retracts, redefines the ministry of women as merely service, and quickly begins to shore up the dykes so that no women may proceed further in ministry than is canonically allowed. Nevertheless lay ministry, especially the ministry of women flourished in all the traditional areas of justice, hunger, homelessness, and all forms of helplessness and exclusion. And this development has not ceased, although many of these ministries have now been cut loose from the official Church. Hospital, school and prison chaplaincies flourish and these institutions often wonder how they could survive without them. Women still have huge difficulties in gaining official recognition and official designation, but that has not stopped them from pursuing their goals, canonical restrictions placed in comparison with biblical mandates. This kind of official Church action has often left women wondering why they need official approval at all, and has only served, on occasion, to remove women further from the heart of the Church.

Again, it is clear that it is women themselves who have taken the initiative here. The official Church has been more discouraging than encouraging, and invokes the principle of ecclesiastical hierarchy – or patriarchy – when faced with women's initiatory choices. The fact that many women are now theologically educated adds to the women's determination and the Church's nervousness. Whenever there is official discussion of the state of the Church, leaders lament the lack of lay participation. It is obvious that they are thinking of men, because women are participating, welcome or not, in their droves.

Behind all this, for better or worse, is the new emphasis on spirituality. Of course there are endless misunderstandings in this area with distorted comparisons between religion and spirituality, but nevertheless, the whole idea of a spiritual dimension to life, of the internalisation of spiritual values, of achieving a biblical spirituality can only be encouraged. When the Vatican directs a movement towards the 'new evangelisation', it is to this biblical basis of all Christian spirituality that it is appealing. There are now great opportunities for ordinary women and men to pursue and deepen their involvement with both personal and communal prayer. The literature on these subjects has increased a thousand-fold, to such an extent that, as Pope Francis himself remarked, the traditional language of official Church documents now leaves many people unmoved. In his recent exhortation, *Evangelii Gaudium*, the pope adopts the role of a spiritual director rather than a teaching Pontiff. And the whole is rooted in biblical spirituality as the very basis of Christian life. For the first time, this pope lays doctrine to one side as secondary and places the gospels front and centre.

There are many other areas of Vatican II influence that have forever changed the face of the Church, like ecumenism, inter-faith dialogue, global ecclesial awareness and many others, but perhaps one of the greatest influences on recent Christian life, side by side with the Council, has been Christian Feminism. Both the Council and Feminism are rooted in the sixties, and both have suffered the ups and downs of succeeding decades. The essential characteristic of all forms of feminism is that it begins with reflection on the experience of women. This, of course, is impossible for all male theologians and philosophers, except in a very indirect way. No male, no matter how brilliant or saintly has ever given birth, and the experience of rape for both women and men has haunted male-female sexual relationships down through the centuries in so many different contexts. This is not the first time that women Christians have turned to their own experience, as we have seen, but it is the first time that the experience of women has been placed in the context of social and religious history and analysed accordingly. When the word 'patriarchy' began to be used in the sixties by Christian feminists, with regard to the Christian Church, there were protesting outcries. But, particularly in the Roman Catholic Church, that structure cannot be called other than patri-archal, and this is proclaimed as the will of God for the Church.

The advent of Christian Feminism gave rise to a whole series of Papal teachings about women, which, in essence, even though there was some blurring of language, simply reiterated the long-standing Church teaching about women's auxiliary role. Initially for feminists and for popes, the attention centred on the subject of women's priestly ordination and this focused the discussion for decades, as well as being a real distraction from the central issues.

Feminism, from its very beginning in the mid-nineteenth century has always followed two streams, a secular and religious expression.

Early secular feminists were intent on obtaining the vote and other rights for women and this emphasis on rights has continued to the present day alongside other newly-developed emphases. Because of the focus on rights, perceived widely as women demanding male rights, feminism was in a confrontational mode. Over the decades some real advances have been made in suffrage, inheritance, economic and labour rights.

The religious stream focused initially on the Scriptures, their translation, interpretation and use in controlling women's lives. Unlike the response to the secular stream, there was, in the Church, only outrage and opposition, not only to women's suffrage, but all other forms of women's rights. All the old chestnuts about women's inferiority were recalled with even more venom, sometimes dressed up in the portrayal of women as weak creatures needing the protection of home and husband. It is obvious that neither the feminists nor the Church's official teachers were aware of the Christian history of women. The First and Second World Wars stalled both feminist streams, but also unknowingly opened up unforeseen avenues, summed up in symbols like 'Rosie the Riveter'. While all the men were at war, the various nations needed women to run the factories and women discovered that they could easily carry out functions that they had previously been told they were quite incapable of performing.

The 1950s saw a return to what was thought to be the traditional roles of women in Church and State, summed up in expressions like 'mom and apple pie'. There was huge pressure on women to be 'home-birds' and to be content with their private family lives. But there was no turning the clock back, and as education was extended to women in several areas, the solely private perception of women was changed dramatically. Initially, the Christian feminist movement, barely recognised as a movement, functioned mainly at the level of academic research. Because of the earlier emphasis on the rights of women, there was still a great deal of focus on ordination, but eventually, the research interests of feminists spread, inspired mostly by the official responses to their initial ever-so-polite requests for attention.

The Second Vatican Council (1962–65) took place in a context that was already changing for women. Women scholars were studying the ancient biblical languages. They were delving into Church History and noticing the total absence of women from the accepted historical accounts. It was entirely possible to produce a twelve-volume history of Christianity without ever mentioning women. Women were studying theology, and their numbers increased dramatically as the population of male theological students began to diminish. What could be seen as an economic choice by many colleges and universities contributed to the theological education of women in revolutionary fashion. It soon became clear that the old seminary theological curriculum did not in any way serve women's theological needs. There are endless hilarious stories about celibate priest-professors trying to explain Catholic sexual morality to women who had mothered several children and who did not recognise the female creatures described in the traditional male theological texts.

As the women scholars pursued their goals, and found each other on campuses all over North America and Europe, and eventually the whole world, they continued their delvings into traditional Church history and theology. Eventually, most theological colleges and universities found that they had to hire such women, whether as an honest recognition of a new form of scholarship or in response to the demands of their women students.

It was the linking of the two words 'lay' and 'ministry' that gradually awakened interest and growing enthusiasm on the ground. As the women scholars scanned each new Council document to see if the Episcopal councilors knew of women's existence, women in parishes and other institutions began to call the work that they were already engaged in 'ministry'. Church teachers rushed to point out that women could not minister, only serve, but the Rubicon had been crossed. Women were told that their enthusiasm was entirely misplaced and that God's will for them had been clearly pointed out from the beginning, 'created second, sinned first'. As the sixties and seventies advanced, the papal and ecclesiastical responses in some quarters became a little less punitive and discriminatory, but the facts remained the same. Women could not teach, preach, minister, or contribute officially from their female experience. Women's place was in the home, or, as the church now taught, in the 'world' and that was where she applied her particular womanly genius, but this was not required in the Church.

For the first time in centuries, however, the official church had to search for a theology that would serve to rule out the religious aspirations of women, and reassert the absolute priority of males as the official leaders and teachers and ordained personnel of the Church, without seeming to insult modern women Catholics. For the old 'inferiority' argument did not work any more. Laws against discrimination against women and others were beginning to be formulated, so the Church was forced to find a new way of expressing their old 'truth'.

While the Second Vatican Council was not at all interested in women in the Church, apart from women in the religious life, and only marginally interested in women in the rest of society, it was eventually the question of the priestly ordination of women that forced ecclesiastical teachers to deal with the 'women problem'. In the early seventies, Pope Paul VI directed the Pontifical Biblical Commission to explore the teaching of the Scriptures for light on this issue. These men, scholars from all over the world, eventually reported that the Scriptures offered no light on the matter of women's ordination, or any ordination for that matter. It was beginning to be understood that the long-standing historical claim that Jesus had personally instituted the sacraments could not stand up to historical exploration. Certainly, theologically, symbolically and spiritually, the sacraments have scriptural antecedents, but these are not literal historical connections.

As it happened, Pope Paul VI chose to ignore the advice of the Commission, and proceeded to write an encyclical against the ordination of women, *Inter Insigniores*, which invoked the 'fact' of the call of only twelve men and the 'fact' that Jesus did not include women. Then an entirely new theology was devised based on the 'maleness' of

Jesus and the necessity for the priest to be like Jesus in his maleness in order to be an *alter Christus*. Other theological conclusions were drawn from the bridal symbolism (the Church is the bride of Christ) in the Letter to the Ephesians, a theology that was always going to cause trouble because it proved too much. It implied that if the Church is the bride of Christ, therefore all men should be ordained to represent Christ and only women should be the recipients of their ministry.

From the moment of the publication of this encyclical, two things happened. First of all, support for the ordination of women proliferated throughout the Catholic Church, among 'ordinary' people who before had not given the matter much thought. Secondly, almost every theological faculty in the world acknowledged that the theology of the encyclical was faulty at many levels, and could not stand up to strict theological analysis. There was, in fact, a third result, the arrival of the anti-feminist movement in the Church and the rebirth of a new kind of Catholic fundamentalism. Despite further efforts by Pope John Paul II to improve the theology, as we have seen, by appealing to women's 'genius' for self-sacrifice and acts of private compassion, the question of the ordination of women has remained a kind of permanent battleground in the Catholic Church. When Pope Francis was asked about ordination, he added his permanent 'no' to the existing nos. The pope could not have done anything else without completely delegitimising his predecessors. As the situation with Pope Francis illustrated, the official Catholic response is now one of authority and theological explanations have been abandoned. It also illustrated that, for whatever reason, the world's media have taken it upon themselves to pursue this question, not necessarily in the interests of women, but in the attempt to get a 'scoop'.

Let us return to the feminists within the Christian tradition, and particularly within the Roman Catholic tradition, since most other Christian Churches and denominations now ordain women. The second wave of feminism in the sixties, rooted as it was in obtaining what were seen as natural rights for women, affected Catholic-believing feminists. Scholars had pointed out the historical and theological invisibility of women and the historically-continuous Christian discrimination against women. They were also beginning to research what women were actually doing throughout Christian history, since women have been present from the very beginning. How did women live? Pray? Worship? How did women see themselves as believers? What did or could women contribute to Christianity? One result of all these questions was a huge corpus of strictly scholarly material revealing the almost forgotten contributions of women. We now know the names and accomplishments of hundreds of women, from disciples to apostles, martyrs to virgins, mystics to heretics, founders of religious communities to missionaries, reformers to inspirational spiritual leaders. Another result was the consequent arrival of ways to disseminate this information, from university courses to the Retreat and Spiritual Direction movements. These were often initiated by religious sisters who had re-examined their own lives and vocations. This resulted in a grass-roots movement of women with a new spiritual outlook and new spiritual and theological resources, some of whom identified themselves as feminists, but all of whom, knowingly or not, benefited from the feminist analysis of Christianity.

The ongoing concern of traditional ecclesiastical theology and papal teaching centred, almost entirely, on women's bodies. It was, in reality quite an extraordinary situation with celibate men teaching women who they were and what their bodies signified. Even though it may no longer have been said in so many words, the ancient understanding that femaleness, the carnal and bodily component of women, was the part furthest removed from the Divine, that understanding still persisted in the official silencing and invisibility of women, and in practices such as mandatory priestly celibacy. As Pope John XXIII remarked, priests should live as if there were no women in the world.

It was not the bodies of women that perturbed the first wave of feminists within the Christian tradition, but the necessity of identifying themselves as part of the Christian community. As the Second Vatican Council seemed to open doors and invite participation, women were repeatedly told that their aspirations were not the intention of the council. These women could eventually be called Christian Feminists. They were totally sure of their Christian identity as women, and they wanted to experience their presence within the Church in a new way. They were trying to make a new Christian space for themselves within a community where they had worshipped, prayed and worked all their lives. But the more they tried to articulate this, the more they seemed to be blocked. Even though most Catholic women were not remotely interested in being ordained to the priesthood, they were shocked at the conclusions of Pope Paul's encyclical. Most people thought that eventually the Church would 'catch up' with the secular world, as women were entering professional education. Becoming scholars in many areas and attaining positions in the professions that had hitherto been unavailable to them, many women just seemed to drift away from the Church. Most women did not understand the reasons for the Church's resistance and certainly had no comprehension of the proffered theological explanation. Many Catholic feminists in the sixties and seventies began to know the meaning of having a broken heart as far as their Church was concerned. Some turned to anger, some just departed from a church they had long loved, but others turned to Christian tradition to explore the sources of women's lives and religious attitudes and also the sources of the Church's resistance to women. Many women, especially Christian feminist women, realised they were no longer welcome in the Church, that their presence there was somehow a major problem in a way they had not perceived before. Many battles were fought over what was called 'inclusive language' at the local level in parishes and other gatherings. Did 'pray my brothers' address only the brothers present, or were women presumed to understand that they were somehow included. As the secular world moved ahead, even legally, from saying 'men' when they meant 'men and women', the writings of official Catholicism persisted, and continues to persist in using exclusively male language in official writings from the Roman Catechism to the revised Liturgy. Pope Francis is a happy exception to this official rule.

After decades of being told that the word 'men' grammatically included women, many women began to realise that it definitely did not and was never intended to. Whatever grammatical points may be made for the history of English, the unwillingness to change soon revealed the depths of the problem of resistance to women. Eventually, a kind of semi-truce happened where, as it was said, on the horizontal level, and where non-official texts were concerned, women were verbally included, but in many cases, this was done not to mark a change in attitude, but to defer arguments. But when it came to the 'vertical' level of inclusive language, an absolute raising of the barricades took place. God was always and everywhere Father, and should be addressed only in male terms. The notion of speaking of God as 'she' sent cold shivers and a *frisson* of horror into the hearts of most Catholics, both women and men. When Pope John Paul I, in his extremely brief time as pope, said that 'God was as truly Mother as God was Father', that statement was mercifully erased by his mysteriously early death. The question of God had moved centre stage and has remained there.

On the other hand, despite broken hearts and ecclesial anguish of many kinds, Christian Feminists were exhilarated as they discovered, in their scholarly research, the real history of women, and the explicit place of women in the Christian scriptures. Jesus had not ignored women and the only official testimony to the foundational events of Christianity, came from the presence and words of women. Christian Feminists discovered their spiritual roots in the heroic women disciples, martyrs, virgins, mystics and missionaries of the past as they raised up to a new awareness a history that had been ignored, buried and counted as insignificant by the male historians of the past. Whatever about the resistance to inclusive language and women's ministry, Christian Feminists, and other mostly women scholars (male scholars quickly realised that pursuing the question of women radically shortened their careers), discovered that they had a Christian history, a legitimate history of the presence and teaching and wisdom of women down through the ages that had been intentionally buried. The seeds of a newly-inclusive Christianity were in their hands and they joyfully took up the task of moving towards this goal.

The scene and context had changed, however. This search was no longer carried on within the confines of the institution, which continued to manfully resist any change in the *status quo* of women. It was no longer a question of ordination but of existence in a community where one was welcomed, respected, treated with dignity and accounted of infinite worth, and where one's voice was listened to and one was expected to contribute to the building up of the community. This is the Third Wave of Christian Feminism, achieved while secular feminism was racing through its third, fourth and fifth waves. Especially during the two papacies of John Paul II and Benedict XVI, the expectation of an eventually-inclusive community decreased radically. There were more and more individual clergy who sympathised with women, saw, in part, what the problem was, but were totally incapable of changing the situation.

And so the age of the Christian Feminist had arrived. In this case, Feminist has become the noun and Christian the adjective, and the lens of observation has changed radically. These women no longer started from the Church and its teaching, but from their own lives and their own experience. Women began to explore their own theological and spiritual resources, rooted in their bodily identity as women, rather than trying to assume a stance imposed by an unsympathetic Church. Instead of trying to pursue a full Christian life on the margins of a male-dominated Church, women chose to put themselves at the centre of a new spiritual reality, and pursue their God and their story from that perspective. This was a completely radical change in Christian self-perception. It was not exclusive of men, but, as it happened, few men were particularly interested. These women realised that an enormous work of Christian reconstruction needed to be done. They knew – and know – that the end result will hopefully be a fully inclusive Church of women and men, but from now on, the women will speak for themselves and not follow an imposed anthropological identity. This entailed a personal commitment to reconfigure minds and imaginations, to re-read the Christian heritage and to take, as the women mystics had done, the *imago dei* as referring specifically to women as well as to men, and not to women through men, as was central to official church teaching. The reality and depth of new convictions led to a change of praxis, and to the building of new communities. Women chose to be a church rather than to try to reform a male church that was impervious to reform, where women were concerned. Exegetes, historians, theologians, spiritual leaders all joined together in search of a life of full womanly Christian integrity. Part of this whole process of womanly reconstruction entailed a global awareness and outreach that gave new resources and raised new hopes. Another Rubicon had been crossed, with the official institutional Christianity practically unaware that anything had happened. This is more or less where we are at the moment and a future of enormous significance remains to be faced.

The Once and Future Church

For about twenty-five years immediately after the death and resurrection of Jesus, the small new Christian community was a fully-inclusive community. Indeed, it seems to have originated, as so often later in history, from the initiative of women. After the men had 'abandoned him and fled', the women disciples remained faithful. They gathered together the scattered remnants of the traumatised followers of Jesus and melded them into a functioning, and eventually missionary, group. Those first twenty-five years seem to have been years of a kind of feverish activity, with women and men apostles, prophets, teachers and preachers racing up and down from Jerusalem outwards, spreading the Good News. By about the year 55 CE, as we have seen, the discriminatory trend set in. It seems that the message of Jesus was not strong enough to counteract the old accepted divisions of Jew and Greek, slave and free, male and female. The community that seemed to have been initiated by Jesus and carried on by the women was now reverting to a patriarchal model, as is evident in the writings of Paul. For about another hundred years, there are signs of a struggle, but by the end of the second century, a male-dominated Church was settling into place.

So is a fully inclusive Church possible again? Pope Francis certainly seems to think so, at least at the level of his personal actions, but many of his followers seem prepared to save the Church from such an inclusive future. They prefer the old divisions between the good and the bad, the rule-makers and the apparent rule-breakers. As for the pope, a true son of Julian of Norwich, even though he does not seem to be remotely aware of her, rule-breaking does not matter. What matters is the acceptance of the *imago dei* at the core of the person, and the recognition that such an image is present in all, without exception.

Apart from the first twenty-five years of Christianity, women have not been accepted as Christians on an equal footing with men. Various official theological explanations have been provided for this state of affairs, starting from the original theological explanation in the first Letter to Timothy (2:11-15): 'For Adam was formed first, then Eve; and Adam was not deceived, but the woman was deceived and became a transgressor.' This explanation has been endowed with apostolic, biblical, and eventually patristic and papal authority, and down through the years has been paraphrased as 'created second and sinned first'. Because of this, women were confined solely to a life of repentance as daughters of Eve, and were considered primarily responsible for the death of Jesus. Down through the centuries some women seemed to outstrip this limiting description of their lives through martyrdom or what was called 'heroic virginity', or other signs of outstanding Christian virtue, but the original theological and exclusionary explanation was always repeated, in case other women got any ideas above their station. In the middle ages, as we have seen, a few extra reasons were added to solidify this exclusion as women mystics and Beguines seemed to excel in Christian virtue, beyond what was expected of them. These reasons included their alleged peculiar proneness to heresy, reading and interpreting the Scriptures for themselves, especially in the vernacular, and daring to teach theological subjects beyond the reach of their fragile minds, such as the doctrine of the Trinity.

After the various inquisitions of the Middle Ages, women were terrorised into silence, and the official Church did not have to deal with their intruding presence until well into the twentieth century. Then a variety of new theological reasons had to be proffered, especially in connection with the claim of some women that they felt a call to priesthood. As a result both priesthood and women received new theological explanations, but the question of women had arrived definitely on the scene, and this time was not going to fade away. For the world had changed. Everywhere women were being educated and making choices about their lives, even their sexual and married lives, for the first time in history. The Catholic Church, in the Western World especially, took on the guise of the one organisation which did not seem to regard women as capable of this behaviour, and therefore as equal members of the community. The official Church tried on new theological explanations which can be summed up in the phrase of Pope John Paul II, 'ontological complementarity', which seems to mean that women, in their very essence, have been created by God to be auxiliary persons, and not full Christian subjects in their own right. This explanation, even if it were known by most Catholics, does not really solve the problem.

And the problem is, as the gospel of Mark pointed out right at the beginning (15:40), 'there were women there'. These are the most revolutionary words for women in the whole of the Scriptures. Women were the solely accepted witnesses of the foundational events of Christianity, because, as Mark has also told us in the previous chapter, all the male disciples had 'abandoned him and fled'. The problem is that women have always been Christians, always been Catholics. They have always been there, and increasingly, they are there in the majority. They are now present as vocal, theologically well-versed members of the community. Women are accustomed to being treated as equals by society, and the incongruity of the Catholic Church's position becomes more and more untenable, whatever the professed theological explanations. Throughout Christian history it has always been recognised that the home is the place where Christianity is passed on, and that women, mothers and grandmothers, have been the prime evangelists. Now in the twenty-first century, homes may no longer function as centres of evangelisation. The old headship of the male husband and father is no longer a reality, and the male leaders of the churches are diminishing in numbers. And yet the women are still there, and this is the problem.

And what of the women down through the centuries? How were they 'there'. As we have seen, they were there among the first and most faithful disciples, as house-church leaders, apostles, teachers, prophets, and presiders at the agape meal, the initial form of Eucharist. They were there, to men's great surprise as martyrs and virgins, not having been deemed capable of either role in male theology. They were there as abbesses and founders, writers and preachers, mystics and scholars, reformers and missionaries, not only at home on the continent of Europe, but in far distant lands, again demonstrating virtues of courage and ingenuity that they were not supposed to have. And in our own time women have been there as theological scholars and biblical exegetes, parish leaders and pastoral guides, chaplains in a huge variety of settings, and ministers of the gospel at bedsides and graves, birthing rooms and schools, publishing houses and universities. And all of this has been done entirely on their own initiative, without any official calling from the Church because the Catholic Church does not consider itself capable of calling women.

And what have these women believed? How have they lived as Christians? What has been the focus of their spiritual lives? Have they seen themselves as the second to be created and the first to have sinned or as more prone to heresy? These women, both today and down through the centuries, right from the beginning, have built their lives around the following of Jesus, the living out of the *imago dei*, the public exercise of compassion and the unique sense of themselves as Godward and God-bearing people. They know that in the depths of their humanity, like Jesus, they discover the signs of divinity. They have learned, as Marguerite Porete, and Teresa of Avila have pointed out, that there is no telling where God ends and we begin, where we end and God begins. They know, as Julian of Norwich did, that there is 'no wrath in God', that God is 'closer to us than our hands and feet', and that God is as truly Mother as God is Father.

They know that the Spirit of God inhabits their lives as tides lurk in the sea, coming and going, rising and falling, but always present. And above all they know that love is the meaning of everything. It is quite extraordinary that Pope Benedict XVI, in his first encyclical on Christian love, never mentions the love of a mother or a father for their child, and never mentions the love that is the central focus of mysticism.

It is obvious that Christianity has travelled through the centuries on two paths, one recognised, acclaimed and celebrated in word and liturgy, the other hidden, often reviled, unrecognised and uncelebrated. If there is to be a future church, these two paths will have to meet. It is not at all clear how this is to be done, but a necessary first step must surely be to attend to the voices of women throughout history and today. Four new women Doctors of the Church have taken their place – with very little pomp and circumstance – on the Christian calendar. That might be a place to start at an official level. But perhaps on an even more important level, the experience of the ordinary day-in, day-out women of Catholicism, can begin to be respected as among the primary bearers of the Faith, and respected, heard and treated as the significant theologians that they are. They can also be recognised and respected as the foundation stones of many a parish community, for without the presence and ministry of women, these communities would not exist. For women have always done theology, and ministry, in both word and deed. Their theology has not necessarily been expressed in tomes or lecture halls, but it is the daily living guide for more than half the Church. This is not to exclude lay men, but at least they can move freely in the male symbolic universe that is Catholicism. Women have had to create their own religious universe, and it is the uniting of these two universes, practically unknown to each other, that will save the Church of God in our time.

A Word about Sources

Since this book is written in a popular vein, I have not appended academic-style footnotes. But the following books will provide adequate information on the contents and sources of the book.

Women & Christianity, Three Volumes, Mary T. Malone, The Columba Press:
 Volume One: *The First Thousand Years*, 2000.
 Volume Two: *The Medieval Period AD 1000–1500*, 2001.
 Volume Three: *From the Reformation to the 21ˢᵗ Century*, 2003.

The Presence of God: A History of Western Christian Mysticism, Five Volumes, Bernard McGinn, The Crossroad Publishing Company:
 especially Volume Three, *The Flowering of Mysticism: Men and Women in The New Mysticism – 1200–1350*, 1998.

A very convenient place to access all recent papal writings on women is:
 Ivy A. Helman, *Women and the Vatican: An Exploration of Official Documents*, Orbis Books, 2012.

The verses quoted in the text are from:
 Mary T. Malone, *Praying with the Women Mystics*, The Columba Press, 2006.